THE LIGHT COMPASS

A guide to finding the route through
to, and understanding of, your soul
in order to achieve intuitive living

Erica Russo

Dedicated to

My Mom and Dad.

For your quiet & unwavering support and for always

doing your best.

CONTENTS

INTRODUCTION

I remember it all too well. I remember the ocean breeze hitting my face as I looked out to the Atlantic Ocean. I remember how cold my tears were when the evening breeze hit my cheeks. I was living a life where I felt lost, confused, and not understanding which way I should turn.

The week prior to this exact moment I asked myself so many questions. "Am I depressed?" "Am I suicidal?" "What the FUCK is happening to me?!"

I felt like I went from being the driver of my life, to being the passenger. I started becoming aware of my surroundings, the people who were in my life, how I was living my life, and how my life as I knew it, wasn't the life I wanted for myself.

I knew I couldn't go back, but I also had NO IDEA what was coming next. For seven days I walked around completely disconnected. I felt numb, but also alive at the same time. Any logical left-brained person would look at this and label it a manic episode. But I wasn't manic. It was different, and to this day I still can't quite explain it, and that says a lot because my Mercury is in Pisces.

I woke up.

Do you know how much work it is to ignite the ignition of a car? It takes more fuel power, more energy, to start the car than it does to drive it for four hours. The one turn of the key starts a domino effect of igniting the engine, turning on all the electrical facilities, starting the antilock brake system, the stereo, the Bluetooth, all of it! One turn of a key [or now press of a button] starts the journey. And all we can do is come along for the ride.

I had my first awakening experience, or 'dark night of the soul' as some would say, in 2017. The experience catapulted me onto my spiritual path. I started practicing a daily meditation, which then led me down the path of Psychic and Mediumship development. If someone were to ask me 5 years ago what my 5 year plan looked like, I would have NEVER in one million years say I'd be a Professional Psychic Medium teaching others to strengthen their connection to spirit while writing a book to assist others in the awakening process and realizing the power they hold.

But one thing I have learned along this wild ride. The Universe is going to put you in places and in circumstances in order to get you to where you need to go. There is no such thing as coincidence, my friend. There are only breadcrumbs. And guess what? You picking up this book is you finding one of those breadcrumbs. You are here right now because you are meant to be here. You listened to the whispers of your soul and ended up here, with me, and man, am I happy to have you!

You see, your intuition, your higher self, your angels, the universe, your ancestors, whatever you want to call it, have been beside you all along. You have been guided by this invisible form/force your whole life. You have had numerous 'breadcrumbs' planted on your path for validation that you are in fact living your purpose.

I wrote this book to act as a lighthouse for you to be your compass as you dive deep into learning about who you truly are and the power that resides within you. This book is a co-creation with Spirit. Many of the words you are about to read came directly from source, from my angels, and from help on the other side. If you read this book, and implement everything you learn into your life – your life as you know it will change. This book is a collection of personal stories, channeled wisdom, and knowledge meant to shift your perception, answer some of your burning questions, and give you some peace as you step into your calling, as you come back to your soul.

Whatever made you decide to open this book, whatever feelings, or gut reactions that led you here, I need you to go ahead and trust them.

And yes, I know how hard that can be. Trusting something that has no tangible proof or validity is crazy right?! It is not logical, it doesn't make any sense, and if we can't make sense of it – how do we trust it?

We trust it by surrendering. We trust it by having faith.

Faith in something far greater than us.

Faith in God.

Faith that the Universe is always looking out for us.

And most importantly, faith in ourselves.

If you are cringing at the idea of having to hold faith, then you are in the right place. If you are grinning from ear to ear screaming "BRING IT ON!" you, too, are in the right place. Wherever you are on this journey, whether you are at the beginning or have been walking along this path for quite some time, you will find something within these pages that you are meant to see. This life you are living and this path you are walking is made to be yours in all of its entirety. Embrace it. Take the tools and wisdom I share with you in the upcoming pages and give yourself permission to shine your fucking light.

I'm happy you are here.

Let's wake up together.

CHAPTER ONE

SOUL

Your soul is waking up. Like a snake, you are shedding the layers of who you thought you were, slowly and perhaps painfully.

Your higher self has started to spend more time connecting with you, using your eyes to see, your mind to think, and your emotions to heal. You might feel worried, or afraid. You might be standing at the edge of a cliff, knowing you can't go back but petrified to take the leap. Before we go on, I need you to know this: you are going to be okay.

When it comes to 'waking up', the first thing you must understand is you are a soul having a human experience. When you become aware of this, your perception of life, your experiences, your troubles, your trauma, it all starts to make sense. Whether you like it or not, you will begin to understand that you chose this life, you chose your gender, you chose your family, and you also chose the lessons that are embedded in your circumstances and events that take place in your life. By all means, your experiences have shaped you into the person you are today. They have been the catalysts in your soul's journey without you ever being aware of them. You have been walking the spiritual path your whole life; you are just now waking up to it. By reading this book, you are taking radical responsibility of your life and I'm not going to lie, I have a girl crush on you.

The woman who understands the power she holds, leans in, and listens to her intuition, uses Spirit as a compass, and finds the lesson in every shitty circumstance, is a woman who is going to change the world. Your soul chose this. However you stumbled across this book, whether it was referred to you by another badass goddess, or maybe it popped up on your Amazon recommendations list, or maybe you found it for fifty cents at a yard sale, it is in your hands now because there is at least one thing in this book that your soul needs you to know. I want these words to find the souls they are meant for. I ask you to highlight the passages and exercises that make a massive impact on you and I want you to write your own wisdom and notes throughout the pages as well.

I then ask you to share this book with a friend, pass it on to someone you know who would grow with the wisdom that is shared. Let's co-create together and raise the collective vibration. Let's wake up.

I have been going back and forth for a while now trying to decide what is the best way to talk about the soul. How do I rationalize a subject so expansive we would never be able to fully comprehend or make sense of its eternal and everlasting power? So, I decided to do the ritual I do prior to any coaching session. I close my eyes, take a couple big deep breaths, bring my hands to my heart and state out loud,

"I am a channel in which Spirit speaks through."

The words alone bring me to a place of peace. Your Spirit, your soul, your higher self, is something you can access at any point in time. It is not something you have to go searching for; it is something you have to remember.

You, as a soul, must remember that the stories you are telling yourself, are simply stories.

You have to remember you hold all the answers within yourself.

You have to remember that you have the capability to access profound spiritual wisdom, healing, and guidance at all times. You do not need a psychic, nor a guru. You are your own guru.

You have the power to create your own reality.

You have the power to manifest all your deepest desires, no matter how scary and far away they may seem.

You just have to get out of your own way.

SITTING IN THE POWER EXERCISE:

Find a quiet, comfortable place where you will not be disturbed for 15 minutes. Allow yourself to be sitting upright in a comfortable position. Close your eyes and allow yourself to attune to your natural breathing. Continue to stay in this place of calm and stillness. Begin bringing your attention to your heart space and envision a white light slowly growing and expanding in your chest. Witness this light as it envelops your whole body. Become aware of how you feel, and the power that is present for you. Stay in this power frequency for the rest of the meditation. Once you are done, write about your experience in your journal. Come back to this exercise whenever you need to.

SOUL'S DESIRES:

Grab your journal, a pen, and a highlighter. Begin writing out all your desires. It doesn't matter what they are, how big or how small, just write them all out. Once you have written out your desires, put your pen down and sit upright with your feet planted firmly on the ground. Bring your hands in prayer position in the center of your chest. State either in your mind or out loud,

"I request to see from the eyes of my higher self."

Once stated, envision a pillar of white light starting at the top of your head and shooting up into the cosmos. Once you feel the connection is complete, open your eyes, take the highlighter, and allow yourself to be guided to the desires you are drawn to. After the highlighting is complete, bring your hands back into prayer position and state out loud or in your mind,

"Thank you for allowing me to see."

And begin closing down the pillar of light. Take a look at the desires highlighted. Allow yourself to be in both student and observer mode. How do these highlighted desires feel for you? Are these desires that you have had for a long time? Do you feel calm or powerful when you read them?

This exercise helps you see just how easy it is to access the point of view of your soul, your highest self. It also is meant to show you that your desires, your dreams, the vision you have for your life were placed in you by a higher force.

The things that light you up are the things that are meant for you.

Now we just need to stop listening to all of the stories we tell ourselves about how we can't have it.

Taking your power back.

Once you understand that your worst enemy is yourself (ego), you start to understand just how powerful your negative thoughts can be on your perception of yourself and in your overall life.

How do we take our power back? How do we stop allowing the ego to control our lives? The answer is simple; we become the gentle observer.

Rather than BELIEVE your thoughts, observe them. Question them. Call them out on their bullshit. Rephrase them to have them be more supportive of your hopes and desires.

Let's think of it this way. There is a car. The car is you. It doesn't matter what kind of car it is. It can be whatever type of car you want it to be. In this car, there is a driver and a passenger.

The driver spends his or her energy driving the vehicle. Being fully aware of traffic signs, the other cars around them, construction on the road, traffic. The driver being the responsible party is going to get annoyed. They are going to feel the frustration of having to deal with reckless drivers, traffic, construction, check points. Let's label these scenarios as 'thoughts'. It doesn't matter if they are positive or negative thoughts.

The driver of the vehicle is going to have a front row seat for everything happening around the vehicle.

When there is a traffic jam, they are the ones feeling the disappointment and agitation. If they get a ticket from a police officer, they are the ones who feel the negative emotion. We feel the thoughts we think.

Now, let us take a different approach to this. Let's say we take ourselves out of the driver's seat and into the passenger side. We are still in the same vehicle, we still have the same destination, but instead of being the driver – we become the observer. As the observer, we are able to see a totally different perspective of the situation. We are able to observe the instances and obstacles along the car ride without situations taking a toll on our mental state. If there is traffic, we might a become irritated but we can quickly snap out of that negative stream of thought because instead of living our thoughts, we are simply just observing them.

When we become the observer, we are able to consciously notice any positive or negative spikes in our mental and emotional state. We can understand exactly what are our triggers are and instead of allowing these triggers to bring on a negative spiral, we, the observer, have the power to let go of any negative feelings or thoughts that come into our conscious mind.

Throughout my life, I never considered myself an 'anxious' person. I never had crippling anxiety to the point where my life had to be put on hold. Of course, being a human being, I did encounter times within my life when I became affected by situations and circumstances where anxiety would pop its nasty little head in, but I would not say I suffered from it.

It was not until I got out of the driver's seat of my mind and placed myself into the passenger seat that I had a front row center view of just how much worry and anxiety were key players in my everyday life. The first day I become the passenger of my life was the day I was able to fully witness my thought patterns and their effects and how they brought no value to my life. I observed one negative thought turn into two negative thoughts, then to three, then it turned into a morning filled with a downward negative thought spiral. I quickly noticed how easy just ONE negative thought could ruin a whole day. Could you imagine the power all your negative thoughts combined can have on your life?

HOMEWORK ASSIGNMENT:

Go to your calendar and choose one day. Circle it, put a star in it, set a reminder on your phone. I want you to fully commit to being the observer of your thoughts that whole day. Have a notebook or journal handy throughout your day.

Wake up 15 minutes early and find a relaxing, comfortable place to sit and quiet your mind for 15 minutes. Close your eyes, and just let yourself be still. Meditation is not about silencing the mind; it's about quieting it. If a thought comes in, simply observe and it and let it pass. Gently bringing yourself back to your breath. After this 15-minute meditation, write down how you feel. Do you feel different from other mornings? Do you feel different from last night? Whatever you are feeling, good or bad, write it down.

Now, go about your normal day. Have breakfast, take a shower, drink your coffee, whatever it is you usually do. Remember, we are observing our behavior and thought patterns today – not living them. Think of yourself as a 'Do It Yourself Mindful Super Nanny.'

WRITE IT DOWN

Every hour, check in with yourself. Set a timer on your phone, write a note to yourself on your hand, whatever it is you need to do remember to take 1-3 minutes at the end of every hour to write down any beliefs or thought patterns you experienced in that last hour.

Did you become annoyed walking into your bathroom to have it be a total mess? Did you feel some judgment towards the woman news anchor whose outfit was not appropriate for daytime television? Did you become anxious and annoyed trying to get your children to the bus stop on time? Did getting stuck behind a slow driver get you irritated? It does not matter how big or small the circumstance was. Write it down. Use the below prototype when journaling:

What occurred?

What emotions did you feel?

How long did those emotions last?

It's crucial to remember to check in with yourself every hour. We must be fully be aware of the emotions and thought patterns we come in contact with on a regular or semi-regular basis in order to be able to transform our thought process and negative patterns.

Throughout your day, try and remind yourself you are the observer, not the owner, of your thoughts. With just this realization, you will feel better. Like most things in life, we have to remind ourselves when a change occurs. How many times have you caught yourself dialing an ex, not because you are lonely and wanting to rekindle the romance, but because it's from pure habit? How many times have you forgotten to put your reusable bags in the trunk of your car and only realized it when your shopping cart was half way filled?

It takes conscious effort to try a different approach. It takes commitment and sacrifice in order to make any type of change. There will be times throughout this exercise that you forget you are the observer. You will get sidetracked from this action and become your thoughts. Don't beat yourself up about it. Just simply put yourself back into the passenger seat.

RECAP

At the end of the day, sit down and reflect on your day of observation. Go through your journal. What occurrences stood out? How many times within the day did you feel a certain emotion? Was there an underlying emotion for a big portion of the day because of an event that occurred?

Don't judge yourself on the results of this exercise. The human experience is made up of thousands of different moods, feelings, and emotions. Becoming the observer gives us a much different approach into analyzing our behaviors and our points of no return. This exercise allows us to pinpoint the thought patterns we want to change and what things we could have handled differently.

We have to make conscious evaluations and notice our triggers, thought patterns, and behaviors that create the energy flow within our lives.

CHAPTER TWO

SILENCE

There is great power that comes from stillness. It is something most people will never experience in their lives. Pure, unattached silence. The ability to be able to dismiss the stories we hold onto, the chatter that is on a continuous loop inside our minds. We have grown so accustomed to stress and worry, and seeking the answers outside ourselves that we forget we have them, stored within the safe confines of the silence most of us are afraid to connect with.

We live in a fast paced, goal-oriented world. We form our thought processes and our belief systems through the ideas that our culture, our society, and the media has put in front of us. We are taught at a very young age how we should act, what we should believe in, and who we should be. We have been told by outside forces, whether they are our parents, our teachers, our peers, or our employers what is right and what is wrong.

The only place we live 100% of our time here in this life is within our own minds. The experienced world traveler and the man who never left his childhood home may have two undeniably different lives, and yet, they both have everything in common. They live their lives through their minds. Everything we experience, every thought, every circumstance, every outlook we have, is the outcome of the miraculous mind. A negative mind will have a negative life – a positive mind will have a positive life. This fact does not discriminate within class systems or life circumstances.

How do we see if our minds are positive or negative? By becoming the observer. If there was mold growing in the far corner of your basement, far away from where you live your everyday life, you would not know there was a problem until you observed it. When you observe the problem, you are able to take responsibility for the problem and do with it what you will. You can avoid the problem and allow it to grow, or you can take the steps to help heal it. The choice is yours.

DON'T HATE – MEDITATE

Writing this book has been such an incredible experience. I have been sitting at my kitchen table in front of my laptop reminiscing on what the practice of meditation has brought me.

It has not only enriched my life with some of the most beautiful and spiritual experiences, opened the door to enhancing my psychic and mediumship abilities, it has also given me the ability to detach and be the quiet observer. And, as much as I love connecting with Spirit, and harnessing my intuition, being the quiet observer is and will always be my favorite take away from meditation.

The simple act of quieting the mind will allow you to see just how cloudy your perception truly is. Being the observer of your thoughts is a totally different experience than being the thinker of your thoughts. Giving yourself the gift of meditation is the most beneficial self-care regimen you can acquire.

Different strokes for different folks.

Ram Dass once said, "The Spiritual Journey is individual, highly personal. It can't be organized or regulated. It isn't true that everyone should follow one path. Listen to your own truth."

Each and every person who has a spiritual practice, has their own unique way of connecting to Spirit. There is no right or wrong way. You can find your solitude in many places and in many different ways. Talking walks in nature, closing your eyes and lighting some candles while soaking in a sea salt bath, sitting outside on your porch as you watch the sunrise with your morning coffee – when you practice truly being in the moment – meditation will become a part of your life without you being aware of it. The act of mindfulness is different for everyone, but still brings all the benefits to anyone who practices it.

Both my husband and I are active meditators. We embarked on our meditation practices together and soon discovered our spiritual paths were quite different. As our practices developed, we ended up taking different directions on our journeys. He enhanced his meditation practice by performing strong determination sitting as well practicing self-inquiry work.

My spiritual path took me in a different direction. As I trained myself to go to a deeper state of silence during my sessions, I started receiving messages from Spirit. As my spiritual practice strengthened so did my psychic abilities. Through my mind's eye, I could see a vivid picture of the spirit I was connecting with and with whom they were trying to get a message to. At first, fear took over and I abruptly would block out any form of communication I was receiving. This went on for months. A lot of this has to do with my very logical mind. We will discuss this more as well as the topic of surrendering in a later chapter.

When you allow your mind to be still, your soul shows up.

When your soul shows up, it brings wisdom and the answers.

It is your job to listen and integrate.

It's really that simple. When we give our higher self the opportunity to speak, it will. Sometimes it will come during meditation. It might show up through intuitive ideas, synchronicities, or opportunities. You will know when it's your soul's doing – just don't let your ego tell you otherwise.

Remembering your power.

Remember the way the smile on your face felt. Remember how your heart felt. Embrace this feeling. Bask in this feeling of glory.

This feeling that you are feeling right now is your birthright.

It is this feeling that will be your sign your soul is speaking to you.

Life is meant to feel good. Life is meant to be happy and to be filled with the things that bring you joy. Joy is the finish line.

CHAPTER THREE

THE CYCLE CONTINUES...

"When it hurts, observe. Life is trying to teach you something." Anita Krizzan

Take a step back and witness your life and the events and circumstances that have unfolded that have brought you to this present moment. Do you notice any patterns or repetitions that have occurred throughout your life?

Relationships. Career. Trauma... It is all trying to teach you something, to bring you closer to your soul and to God. As heart breaking as some circumstances are, when we have the understanding and acceptance of our own spiritual obligations and the divine existence of unconditional love, we hold the power and wisdom that will allow us to thrive in negative circumstances.

Have you ever known someone whose life is a stream of the same core problems manifested into different situations and people? Have you ever caught yourself in a moment that felt far too rememberable?

Spirit will keep on giving you the same lessons over and over again until the lesson is learned.

It is very hard to see these patterns and repetitions while we are engulfed in them. This is where things like meditation and journaling come in handy. It is in the stillness, when we begin to feel the power of our soul.

As spiritual beings we have the power to attain greatness. Each and every soul has the God-given right to manifest our reality. It is our choice if we see the glass as half empty or half full.

While we are on the topic of cycles and patterns, I want to touch on a personal story of mine. My dear friend Kayla is one of the nicest people I have ever known. She is one of the most patient and devoted parents I have ever met, and she brings laughter and happiness to any conversation. For the whole of her life, Kayla has encountered repetitive patterns within her romantic relationships.

Her first marriage ended as she found out her husband had been unfaithful. This left Kayla in absolute shock and made her question her own part in the dissolution of her marriage. After the divorce was final, Kayla started dating a younger man; we will call him Dan. Dan and Kayla decided to move in together and take their relationship to the next level. Throughout their courtship, Kayla noticed traits of Dan's that were very similar if not identical to her ex-husband's. He would question her loyalty and became extremely paranoid when other men would strike up a conversation with her. He would passive aggressively remark on her demeanor when other men were around. This behavior was a dose of déjà vu for Kayla. She had lived it in her marriage.

Kayla and Dan's relationship continued and now they are the parents of two young children. Through the years, Dan's behavior still mimicked that of her ex-husband. It wasn't until her sister-in-law confronted Kayla with news regarding distrust and infidelity that Dan had committed that she had to face the truth. As Kayla digested this information, it did not dawn on her this was, in fact, the same situation she had encountered with her ex-husband nine years prior. It was her ego that brought her to a place of blaming herself for the behavior of her partner, just as she did in her previous relationship.

As my friendship with Kayla grew, so did my consciousness. As I learned about her past, I couldn't help but notice the vast similarities between her two relationships. I saw how distraught she was when she learned about Dan's indiscretion in relation to her, and I wondered how one could endure going through the same pain twice! I took it upon myself to point out the pattern unfolding. I gave her a quick overview of how the Universe puts obstacles in front of us to help us learn and to grow. It wasn't until then she realized these relationships were lessons for her.

My point is this. It takes an outsider's perspective to notice the cycles occurring within your life, and now YOU can be the outsider. We cannot rely on others to point out these patterns and to be honest, we might not want to hear them from others. We must become the non-judgmental observer of our life's journey. The way we do this is by silencing the mind and taking a step back.

Our journeys are so unique, so inspiring, and so custom designed. Wherever you are on your journey at this moment, you have already learned many lessons and have climbed many mountains. You have already been through at least 100% of the worst days of your life.

EXERCISE:

Take a moment and write down 3-5 life lessons you have already learned. Then give yourself a big hug because of what you are doing, because you are amazing and you can be justifiably proud of yourself.

Follow the yellow brick road.

If I sat here and told you once you begin a meditation practice, all your problems will cease to exist, I would be lying. Pain, sorrow, anger, anxiety will still be there; they will still linger and pop their ugly little heads in, but the power they have over us will decrease significantly. When we quiet our minds, we give ourselves the opportunity to detach from those thoughts that lower our vibrational state.

I am not going to sit here and tell you what you will encounter as you begin to silence your mind, and to clear the connection to your soul, because truthfully, nobody knows.

Whether you are on the path towards enlightenment, or creating a bridge between two realms, your spiritual path is unique and custom built for you. Trust the process, and allow Spirit to guide you in the direction that is meant for you.

MASTERING MINDFULNESS

Mindfulness is defined as:

'Paying attention in a particular way: on purpose, in the present moment, and non-judgmentally.'

So, what does this exactly mean? It means instead of allowing your mind to wander, which it has a natural instinct to do – it means to practice being fully present, in the moment. The concept is that simple; the practice of it is not.

We tend to either think about the past or jump into the future. We reminisce on past events and regrets, and we worry about potential future outcomes. Being fully present in the moment takes hard work and commitment. It takes willpower and a strong determination to be fully committed to understanding the power of now.

Our minds are constantly moving, living beings. Let's look at our minds as though they are fields. Whether they are filled with wildflowers or land mines is ultimately up to us.

When we allow ourselves to be fully present in the moment, we block our minds from going to the places that start the negative spiral of thoughts. We do not allow ourselves to sit in past events we wish to critique and analyze. We do not allow anxiety to build up about future events that have not even occurred yet. We are just in the now. We are fully present.

Mastering the art of mindfulness is not easy. Truthfully, I believe it to be the hardest practice one can acquire.

Our minds are insane, fast-paced, constantly moving hyperactive monkeys on Ritalin. They do not stop, they do not sit, they do not rest. They are absolutely exhausting. Have you tried to calm down a hyperactive monkey on Ritalin? How about an energetic two year old? They'll calm down for a couple minutes, but then they are back to wreaking havoc.

Now imagine trying to tame this monkey every day for the rest of your life? Sounds pretty hard, yes? That's because it is. Yet, the benefits of practicing mindfulness are far greater than allowing the Ritalin infused monkey to run amuck.

It takes years of practice and commitment to be fully present in the moment. Even the most well-seasoned meditators still become lost in the train of thought at times. It is the discipline and kindness you give to yourself that allows you to simply come back to the moment.

Whenever and whatever that is, allow yourself to notice the behavior, and then try to gently, bring yourself back to the present moment.

MINDFULNESS EXERCISE:

A simple and effective way to practice mindfulness is by starting off at meal times. As you sip your morning coffee, feel the mug around your hands, smell the aroma as it hits your nostrils. Take your time and notice subtle notes of different flavors as you swallow. Pay attention to the experience – and don't allow your mind to starting making your daily to-do list.

The same goes for lunch and dinner. Chew your food. And I mean really CHEW your food. Hear the crunch of the lettuce, taste the spices, the herbs, and allow your meal time to be an experience and not just a means of nourishment.

You will quickly notice how easily your mind will wander. How hard it is to stay in the present moment, being mindful of your actions. As I stated before, mastering mindfulness is not going to happen quickly. It's a lifelong process that requires commitment. Be easy on yourself. Don't get pissed when your mind wanders, because, trust me, it is going to.

What is right and what is wrong

'I feel like I am doing it wrong,' is one of the most popular reasons beginning meditators quit. Here is the thing, there is no such thing as doing meditation wrong! It is called meditation practice, not meditation perfect. This is the beauty of it. Your time spent in the quiet is your time to spend sitting with your soul. Whether it is sitting upright in a sturdy chair, laying down on a yoga mat, sitting on a busy train – there is no right or wrong way to quiet the mind.

It is not meditation perfect, it is meditation practice.

This journey is yours and only yours. Bask in the power of the Universe however you like. Whether it be sitting before an altar, laying down in the comfort of your bed with your arms crossed on your chest, hiding in the hall closet for five minutes while closing your eyes and focusing on your breath, it all works.

The stress epidemic

The 21st century has brought extensive growth in technology, knowledge, and business expansion. We are reaping the benefits of the vast collection of new technologies and opportunities that for a very long time were not available to us.

From microscopic surgery procedures, to being able to browse the web, send out an email, have a conversation all within the confines of a four inch metal rectangle (the cell phone). Yet, through this massive growth and evolution of our society, the stress epidemic has grown at the same speed. Stress is such a problem that when we don't feel a continuing underlying stream of stress, we start to create stress. It has become a constant within our lives. It is probably the easiest thing in the world to become addicted to, since there are no external items necessary in forming an addiction to stress.

If you are thinking thoughts about finances, then your reality will be all about finances and the lack of it.

If you think about how unhappy you are in a relationship, your reality is going to be you are in an unhappy relationship.

Want to know why our egos are so powerful? It's because they are invisible. They cease to exist. You are battling an invisible monster. Think of the ego as a mega super villain. Its power is manipulation and its weapon of choice is stress. What a powerful weapon this is. It's silent, it's ongoing, and can take any form. How do we conquer a villain with this amount of power? If we stay attached and stay focused on the fight, we will die trying. Our energy and will to win will eventually diminish and our ego will walk away with a victory.

The best way to deal with a villain like the ego is to detach from it. Just like a narcissistic relationship, the only way to win is to walk away. With the understanding we are not our thoughts – we diminish the power the ego has. Instead of one simple rain drop to turn into a hurricane, we observe the thought and let it pass.

Stop holding onto things that don't make you feel good.

It is your birth right to feel good. It is your free will to choose what thoughts and ideas you are going to hold onto to create your reality. Just like Glinda said to Dorothy,

"You've always had the power my dear. You just had to learn it for yourself."

Clearing out the clutter

I love a good purge. Twice a year I take a week and go through my whole house and go through everything and donate or throw out things no longer serving a purpose in my life. The feeling I have after going through my entire home and getting rid of things feels so invigorating!

Whether you have lived in your home for two years or 40 years – you accumulate stuff. We are natural collectors, just like our ancestors, in not only physical things but non-physical things as well. Now shift your focus on all the thoughts and ideas you have collected through your life.

How many childhood memories can you recall?

How many fears do you have that were acquired at an early age?

How many phones numbers or addresses can you think of off the top of your head?

How many of your teachers or college professors can you name?

How many movies or reruns of TV shows can you mouth every single line perfectly?

Our minds are personal computers. Download after download we collect information that sits in our minds. Can you imagine what this looks like? It most likely looks like an episode of *Hoarders.*

Just like we clean out our cars, our energetic fields, and our houses – we need to remember to clear out our minds as well. We are living our whole lives through our minds, are we not? We might as well make it a nice play to be.

Clearing Meditation:

Start by finding a comfortable, quiet spot. Close your eyes and allow your body to release all the tension and stress of the day. Bring your attention to your breath, noticing the inhale as the air flows into your body and fills your lungs, and the exhale as it escapes through your nose. Allow yourself this time to observe any thoughts that come into your mind, gently pushing them away and coming back to your breath. As you reach a level of quiet within your mind, start envisioning a house before you. What type of house is it? Is it a cottage in the woods? A villa in France? A townhome? As you focus your attention on this house, start walking up to the front door. The door is unlocked and ready for you to open. As the door opens wide, you see countless boxes stacked up high from floor to ceiling. Each box is labeled something different and all symbolizing a thought, memory, or feeling you hold.

From a distance you notice a stack of large boxes that are titled stress, worry, anger, and guilt. You make your way towards this pile of boxes with a red permanent marker. As you approach the stack you notice the difference in size these boxes are compared to the others and the amount of space they require. With the bright red marker, you write the word 'TOSS' on the first box labeled 'GUILT'. You then make your way up to the second box labeled 'ANGER' and write the word 'TOSS' in big capital letters on it as well. You then meet with the box labeled 'WORRY' and write the word 'TOSS' in big capital letters. The more you do this, the lighter you feel. As you make your way to the last box in the stack, you come eye to eye with the box labeled 'STRESS'.

As you write the letter 'T' you feel like a weight has been lifted off your shoulders. As you write the letter 'O', you feel the negative energy releasing its hold on you. On to the letter 'S', you feel the negative energy melting away as it travels down into the ground.

As you write the last letter 'S', you feel an intense energy shift within you, and a stream of positive energy rush through you as it fills your entire body making its way down to the tip of your toes to the top of your head. You see the boxes become transparent until they disappear altogether.

You then walk around the room to look at the other boxes taking up space. The boxes come in different sizes and are labeled different things. There are boxes that say 'childhood memories', 'hobbies', 'achievements', 'dreams' – you notice a corner of the room filled with boxes with large question marks on them that take up a large portion of the room. You make your way to them with the red marker in hand and go through each and every box with a question mark on it and write 'TOSS'. As you take a step back after labelling each and every miscellaneous box – you see them slowly disappear into thin air.

You take a look around the room to see how much more space you have acquired. The room is now filled with clear, white energy that allows you to feel the gratitude of your hard work. You close your eyes and bring your hands to your heart to feel your heart filled with unconditional love and light.

As you come to the end of this meditation practice you start to bring your attention back to the present by wiggling your toes and fingers, taking a deep breath in as you softly open your eyes.

'To make the right choices in life, you have to get in touch with your soul. To do this, you need to experience solitude, which most people are afraid of, because in the silence you hear the truth and know the solutions.'

--Deepak Chopra

The concept of allowing our soul to speak is simple. Make your monkey mind shut up. That's it. That is the magical anecdote for seeking the answers and guidance we all want. Yet, the processing of silencing the mind is not simple. It requires dedication and perseverance. It requires a strong desire to WANT to connect to one's higher self, to Spirit, to a power far greater than us.

Our lives and our minds are so busy that it is easy to forget to check in with ourselves (meaning our souls). Our souls are constantly trying to grab our attention. Our higher selves WANT to help us, they want to see us succeed in our life purpose. Our connection to our soul is through our intuition.

Albert Einstein once said,

"The intuitive mind is a sacred gift and the rational mind is a faithful servant. We have created a society that honors the servant and has forgotten the gift."

Slowly, but surely, we are beginning to see the light in between the cracks of the foundation society has built around us. We are beginning to question, we are beginning to see things for what they are and not want we are being told they are. We are beginning to remember that energy doesn't lie and sometimes salt looks like sugar.

We are beginning to remember that the only person walking this Earth that knows what is best for you, is you.

We are beginning to see the old world come into the new. Where Mother Earth was our medicine, and the wise ones were the witches and mystics that were shunned and cut off for knowing the power that resides within them.

We see it clearly now. We see that we are starting to understand rationalization is one of the many tools of ego-ic mind state.

When strengthened and respected, our intuition is our greatest super power. We have the resources of scholars and prophets at our very disposal. We have the power to end suffering, fear, and hate. The collective consciousness has the underlying power within us to change the world for the better.

We just have to make our egos shut the hell up.

CHAPTER FOUR

INTUITION

The soul speaks, are you listening?

The soul knows, are you trusting it?

The soul allows you to stay divinely guided.

It is that subtle whisper we question.

It is the clear knowing that makes us feel strange.

The soul speaks through our emotions.

It tells us when we are close and when we have strayed away.

It has given us a compass, and left breadcrumbs along the way.

The soul is the wind through our hair immediately after we ask for a sign.

It is the book that manifests at the perfect time.

The soul is the natural comfort you find when you visit your favorite place.

It is the embrace of a loved one after a long day.

The soul speaks through your enlightened ideas,

While creating space for you in the silence.

Your soul does not have to be found,

It has to be remembered.

Your soul has been with you the entire way,

Watching you experience life.

Watching you learn, grow, and heal.

Your soul has never left.

Your soul is waiting for you to answer the call.

It is patiently waiting to entangle itself into your life,

It is here for you whenever you need it.

It is the power that resides within you making you capable of moving mountains,

And overcoming the battles you fight within yourself.

It is the gentle reminder you are perfect just the way you are.

It is the knowing beauty is within.

It is the strength you don't believe you have.

It is the subtle whispers of hope in the darkest of times.

It is the light peeking through when you have been encased in darkness.

It is the breath of fresh air in your lungs.

It is the tears of joy running down your cheek.

The soul speaks, are you listening?

BECOMING INTUITIVE

Where do I begin? I guess a good place to start is at the beginning. I was always a sensitive child with my heart on my sleeve. I was a loner by nature and enjoyed spending most of my time in the woods behind my childhood home. I was fortunate enough to live in a place where nature was in abundance and all I had to do was go outside. I remember seeing things from the corner of my eye as I walked through the woods behind my childhood home. I would pretend there was a Native American Spirit who would collect water in the stream that ran through these magical woods. I'd spend hours swinging on a disc hung on a tree in my front yard because it was the only place where my mind could find peace.

When I hit middle school, I fell onto hard times. Rumors were spread about me, and the hallways of my middle school were the unfriendliest and darkest places in my life. I had death threats jammed into my locker with the subtle words 'KILL YOURSELF BITCH' with a stick figure hanging from a noose, laying on top of my social studies textbook before 6th period in 6th grade. I had the main mean girl come up to me at lunch time as I sat alone at the loser table and tell me she was going to snap my neck in half if I kept looking her way. When I tried reporting her to the lunch aids and then to the social worker, nobody believed me. When asked, she denied ever making the threat.

I would spend countless hours in the guidance department hiding from the torture my peers gave me on a daily basis. I found places within the building that were quiet, and away from the noise. It was during these times, I have never felt so alone. It was during this time, at the ripe age of 14, where I would sit and ponder the best way to commit suicide.

From the ages of 14 to 17 my life was a blur. During these years I had three psychiatric hospital stays, went to two different alternative schools, and was a shell of the person I once was. I reflected the unkindness the world showed me upon myself and because I was sensitive by nature, the only way I could withstand living in such dense, chaotic energy was to shut it off. And so I did.

I shut out the very thing that made me, me. I started to believe the stories my doctors and therapists were telling me. I started to take the pills prescribed to me for my feelings of emptiness and dread. I'd spend an hour every Thursday evening with my therapist. I'd go to the psychiatrist the first Tuesday of the month for a "checkup" to see if the Zoloft and/or Celexa that I was prescribed was working.

I remember sitting in the shrink's office staring at the immense amount of house plants he had scattered throughout the room on various bookshelves and hanging from the ceiling. He had a Hibiscus plant facing the window. As the flower collected the beams of sunlight from outside; it was in that moment I realized, I haven't actually felt an actual emotion in over a year. My highs weren't that high and my lows weren't low. It was like I was in a boat on a millpond. I was in neutral all the time.

There was no healing taking place during these three years. There weren't any revelations or times of acceptance and growth. Because of my age, I was being told what pills to take and what my problems were. The external world was trying to 'fix' an internal problem. During this time and the countless sessions I had with licensed professionals, not one of them told me that I am not my thoughts. Not one of them told me the way people treat me is how they feel about themselves. Not one of them taught me mindfulness or how to connect with my soul. For them, I was just another angry teenager and another prescription.

In early October of my senior year at my alternative school, my inner voice got louder. Something shifted within me. I was tired of running away from my problems and wanted to prove to myself and to everyone else I could graduate from my own school district with my own class with whom I went through kindergarten to 7th grade. The nurturing inner voice within me kept telling me this three year storm I was in, was going run out. The rainbow was waiting for me. I told my parents I wanted to enrol back in my regular school district. I wanted to graduate with my class.

I wanted to prove to myself I was strong and I could handle being with the people who tried to break me down.

And that's what I did.

Three weeks before my senior year graduation, I started dating a guy with a Guido haircut, who drove a piece of crap electric blue Ford Focus and worked before and after school at a local deli. He wrestled, played football, and would throw parties at hotels in neighboring towns. He was popular and well liked. He showed me kindness when nobody else did. He would say "Hi" to me in the hallways, even though I walked through them with the ultimate resting bitch face. After school, he would invite me to the deli he ran, and would be make me turkey sandwiches on day old rolls. This guy ended up being the rainbow at the end of the storm. This guy, ended up being my best friend, my rock, my husband.

This was the first big moment of my life that I listened to my intuition, my inner voice, even when the idea of enrolling myself back into my school district made me absolutely terrified. The idea of willingly putting myself back into a position to be shamed, mistreated, and broken down once again made absolutely no logical sense. Yet that inner knowing, that subtle, almost silent voice within me kept telling me that everything would be okay and everything would end up working out.

I have read so many books on intuition, I have watched so many documentaries, I have taken so many courses and programs on the topic, and yet, I will honestly tell you the best teacher when it comes to intuition and inner knowing, is life itself. If you take a step back and see the timeline of your life and the experiences you have had – you will see your intuition has been naturally woven into some of the most profound and enriching experiences you have had the pleasure to take part in. Your intuition put you exactly where you needed to be at exactly the right time in order for your life to unfold as it has.

The biggest obstacle in allowing yourself to live more intuitively is learning to trust it. Learning to lean into it even when your conscious mind wants to rationalize and tear it apart. Raise your hand if you ever had a gut feeling or intuition about something, you doubt it or don't listen to it, and then something occurs where you end up screaming,

"I FUCKING KNEW IT!!"

Now that everyone's hand is raised, I want you to go ahead and give yourself a quick tough love tap on your forehead. Why? Because you are human. Because deep down hidden behind all of the stories, the lies, the entanglements, is the knowing you have held all along.

Your intuition is your connection to your higher self, to source, to God, to everything that is. It is your Internal Guidance System. Let's think of it this way. Think of every person on this planet being an automobile. Each and every automobile comes with its own Internal Guidance System, like GPS, but better. Some of the cars will have a natural ability to quiet the engine (the mind) and tap into the internal guidance system naturally and with ease. They do not allow the outside world and the traffic around them to influence their connection to their IGS. Other cars will have a harder time tuning into their IGS because they are preoccupied with what is happening around them. Their IGS is still there, they are still equipped with it, but they have a harder time hearing it because of the noise of their own engine and or the chaos of the outside world. Then you have cars that are fucking morons that ONLY listen to the sound of their own engine and the outside world and end up running their asses off the road, flicking people off, and causing unwanted and avoidable circumstances.

Whatever car you are right now, know that investing in this book and reading it, is the first step to getting to having your Internal Guidance System be your number one ally. In anything, the first thing you need to create change is the desire to create change. In the next section of this chapter, I'm going to be sharing 100 ideas to help you live more intuitively. You don't have to do all of them, unless you want to be a bad ass, but allow the process of choosing be based on your intuition. Do the things you are naturally drawn to; don't overcomplicate it. Have fun with this experience and remember your intuition; it's there! You just have to quiet your monkey mind to listen to it.

Exercise: Achieve your basic psychic level

Relax in a quiet place, as in the previous exercises.

Close your eyes.

Visualize a spiral staircase with ten steps curving down to the bottom floor.

Visualize yourself standing at the top of this staircase.

Take a step down to the ninth step and mentally say, 'Deeper psychic level.'

Then take another step down to the eighth step and mentally say, 'Deeper psychic level.'

Continue descending the steps as just described.

When you reach the bottom step, mentally say, 'I am now at a strong psychic level.'

Continue descending the steps as just described.

When you reach the bottom step, mentally say, 'I am now at a strong psychic level that I can use for successful psychic performance. I can reach this level whenever I wish, with my eyes closed or open, simply by desiring to be here and counting from three down to one.'

Open your eyes.

33 WAYS TO LIVE INTUITIVELY

1. Meditate for 15-20 minutes each day.

2. Be barefoot outside as much as you can.

3. Create a playlist that feeds your soul. Put it on shuffle and intuitively guess the next song that comes on.

4. Download ESP Trainer on your phone and play it in those small pockets of time you have during your day.

5. Lie on Mother Earth (naked if you can). Put a timer on your phone for 20 minutes and feel her energy as you blend with her. Be present in the experience.

6. Allow your intuition to guide you with your diet. If you feel like going meat free for a month, or to stop eating a certain food, listen to it.

7. Drink Mugwort tea (it tastes like shit, so you can intuitively create your own blend by adding peppermint, rose, or other dried herbs to make it taste better).

8. Experience a cacao ceremony.

9. Take a breathwork class.

10. Listen to Binarial Beats.

11. Have an energy healing session.

12. Buy yourself an oracle deck you are drawn to, and pull a card a day.

13. Immerse yourself in water under the moonlight.

14. Listen to the warnings and red flags your soul sends you.

15. Go to a local crystal store and without reading the definition, choose the stones you are naturally drawn to. When you're home, check the meanings and see how they are the perfect stones for you during the present time.

16. Go to the farmer's market and buy a fruit or veggie that is organic and fresh; then go to your local supermarket and buy that same item. When you get home make sure you are able to decipher the farm fresh product from the mass produced one by poking a hole into it or something along those lines.

Take the first piece of produce and hold it in both hands while you begin to close your eyes and focus on your breath. Set the intention to feel and/or experience the energy of the item. Once you have done this, do it with the other one. Take note of what you experienced. Have others in your home do the same!

17. Similar to 16, gather herbs and crystals and a notebook. Find a place where you will not be disturbed, possibly under a tree. Allow yourself to be open and receptive to the energy around you. Start by taking one item at a time, holding it in your hands, close your eyes and attune to the energy of this object. How does the energy make you feel? Do you feel confident and proud? Protected? Do you feel feminine or masculine? Don't worry about what the books tell you each of these herbs and crystals mean. Figure out what they mean TO YOU. Write all your impressions down in your notebook.

18. Clear your chakras with crystal healing, chanting, or meditation.

19. Stop and really smell the roses.

20. Fill your life with things that light you up.

21. Create an altar dedicated to your spiritual and personal growth.

22. Pray daily.

23. When you have a download or a beautiful idea come into your awareness, don't question it. Just do it.

24. Re-parent your inner child. Start giving her the love and support she needs to step into her next level version.

25. Dance in the rain.

26. Use the power of your intention by performing an easy intention ritual by holding a seven day candle, closing your eyes and envisioning your third eye, your connection to Spirit, God, your angels deepening and becoming more clear. As you hold the candle in your hands, infuse your intentions into it. Then, light it and place it on your altar.

27. When no one is home, turn off all the lights, light some candles, and burn some incense. Get naked, put on a playlist that moves your soul, and allow the power of your Spirit to guide your movements.

28. Go to your local grocery store and before walking in, take a moment to close your eyes and take a couple big deep breaths. Get into a place of stillness where your thoughts become silent. Send a thought out to your higher self with the request to be guided to the flowers your soul needs at this moment for healing.

Allow yourself to take a couple more deep breaths and then make your way to the florist section. Don't question the experience, just allow yourself to be naturally guided to the flowers right for you at that moment in time.

29. Practice mindfulness.

30. Give yourself the love you desire.

31. Don't overcomplicate things.

32. Name your ego and when the negative bitch shows up, assertively tell her to shut up or sit down.

33. While driving on a country road (or one that isn't busy), use your intuition to guess the next car that will pass by. What color is the car, what make is it, are there certain letters or numbers in the license plate? Remember, exercises like this one isn't about getting it right, it's about flexing your intuitive muscle. It's showing your guides, the Universe, Source, God, whatever you like to call it, how dedicated you are to your growth and connection.

CHAPTER FIVE

HEAL

Close your eyes, put out your hands, and I want you to visualize holding a juicy lemon. I want you to feel the smooth texture as well as the indents of the pores. Now I want you to go ahead and envision a sharp knife cutting through this juicy lemon and seeing the juice drip down the knife. Take a piece of this lemon and visualize it between your lips.

I want you to taste the bitterness of the lemon's citric acid as it hits your tongue.

Notice what is going on in your mouth at this moment. Are you salivating? Did you have to swallow after you experienced the lemon as it touched your tongue?

You just manifested an experience just by thought form alone.

That is how powerful your thoughts are.

We seldom take the time to actually take a step back from our lives to observe how our thoughts create our reality.

Everything is thought.

I want you to go back in time and think of a memory that brought you negative emotions. As soon as this memory comes in, I want you to take note of it, and then drop it. Don't put any more effort or energy into it.

Now I want you to close your eyes and take a deep breath. Go ahead and think of a happy memory. It doesn't matter if it is from your childhood or last week. Go ahead and bring yourself back into this memory. Notice the clothes you are wearing, the weather, go ahead and take note of the smells that were in the air. I just want you to be in that moment. Take note of what emotions are present for you at this time. Go ahead and FEEL what this moment felt like to you. Then gently bring yourself back to the present moment.

What you did was to take two different thought forms and put a different amount of your energy into both, a negative thought form, and a positive thought form.

Between the two thought forms, which one brought out a stronger experience? If you said it was the positive thought form, you are absolutely right. Do you want to know why? Because you put more of your own energy into it.

The human mind will have nearly 70,000 thoughts in a 24 hour period. Some of these thoughts are good, some bad, and some are indifferent. Each thought comes with equal opportunity. It is our choice to choose the thoughts we put our intention and energy into. That is where our power lies.

Your healing will not come when the sun shines upon your face;

It will not come in those times when you experience joy, love, or happiness.

Your healing will occur in the darkness.

When you cannot see the light at the end of the tunnel.

It will be in the times of fear and sadness.

Your healing takes place in the resistance of love.

It will feel like giving up.

It is in the darkness that we grow, both physically and spiritually.

It is in the darkness that truths are discovered.

It is in the black of the night that your soul steps in.

One must undergo many dark nights to reach the highest point of the sunrise.

One must overcome everything they believed would break them, in order to understand the depth of one's strength.

Your healing will come when it is time.

It will come in waves and sudden flashes.

It will come when your mind is silent and still.

It will come when you do not believe yourself to be ready.

Healing is a very human thing.

And it is one's choice on how to heal.

One must not be afraid of the healing process,

You must rejoice in it.

You must become one with your healing.

You must not fight it,

Or turn against it.

You must be patient with it,

And take the time to understand it.

You must make peace with it.

And know you are whole even when you are healing.

WHAT IS A HEALER?

The term healer is a very popular label within the Spiritual community. For the longest time, I did not understand what the term actually meant. Does this mean I should be working in the medical field? Should I have followed in my grandmother's footsteps and become an RN? I spent years trying to understand the definition of a healer. What it meant to BE a healer. Through years of self-discovery, and helping other healers shine their light and strengthen their connection to Spirit, I have created my own definition of HEALER I would like to share with you.

A healer is someone who has the ability to turn trauma into wisdom.

She is one who experiences pain and takes the necessary action to heal rather than to fix.

She finds comfort in nature, and is often times drawn to the water, because of its natural healing abilities.

She understands her divine nature and listens to the whispers of her soul.

She often times will feel like an outsider at an early age because she lives in a world where most need healing, When she is the one who heals.

She holds the mind of an eternal student, for in knowledge comes wisdom, and within wisdom comes healing.

She has a natural ability of making one feel safe and seen.

She radiates a vibrant green aura.

Healers walk among us in many different professions.

Some wear scrubs, others cut hair.

Some are teachers, others are Spiritual readers.

When it comes to being a healer, it is not about what you do.

It is about who you are.

You're a healer at the soul level,

You have been a healer for many lifetimes.

Being a healer does not exempt you from life's pain,

It does not offer you any get out of jail tickets,

You experience trauma just like everyone else.

But you take the pain you have experienced,

And you become the Phoenix, rising from the ashes.

Some hearts are guided to sell out big venues and speak their message to the masses; other hearts are guided to helping this planet in other ways that appear smaller to human eye but are energetically just as important.

Whether you are the person with ambitions of selling out stadiums, or the person who wants to touch people's hearts and open their minds in a smaller more intimate setting – your job remains the same.

You, my fellow lightworker – are here on this earth, at this time, reading THIS because you have been called to be here. To help those in need of light, to help spread love, joy, and hope to humanity.

You are meant to listen, and to console.

You are here to rub backs and heal hearts.

You are here to be the voice of reason, the carrier of hope.

You are here to take care of people, physically and mentally.

You are here to be the friend one calls at 3am.

You are here to lighten up the mood.

You are here to offer a kind smile.

You are here to offer praise and recognition.

You are here to give really amazing hugs.

You are here to sit quietly and listen, with no judgment.

You are here to say something really funny when someone is wanting and can't stop crying.

You are here to open the door to a complete stranger.

You are here to pay it forward on the drive thru line at Starbucks.

You are here to hold a lot of hands.

You are here to experience trauma and loss.

You are here to express gratitude — and recognize when it is missing.

You are to go through troubles and grow through trauma.

You are here to face your fears and speak your truth no matter how hard that might be.

You are meant to a beacon to those who are in need of light.

You are here to help thy neighbor.

You are here to observe your life and find where healing is needed.

You are here to offer advice and guide those who are lost.

You are driven to help, to heal, and to nurture.

You are here to shine your light.

You are here to be the lighthouse.

When I was younger, I used to think being *Tiffany Tough Tits* was how you showed the world just how strong you were.

My beliefs looked something like this:

The bitchier I was, the less of a chance I would have of someone bullying me, jumping me, or spreading rumors about me.

The angrier and meaner I seemed, less and less people would approach me wanting to be kind or friendly, which I believed were just fake attempts anyway.

Bratty behavior, bitchy remarks and a chip on my shoulder kept me safe but got me nowhere. I was a walking open wound. I spent all of my energy creating layers of protection, hiding behind the Hollister Shirts, fake tans, and hoop earrings, when inside, I felt unworthy, unloved, unlikable, and utterly alone.

Here are some things we have to remember: just because someone carries the weight of the world well, doesn't mean it isn't heavy. Just because someone acts tough, doesn't mean they are aren't hurting.

Real strength comes from vulnerability. It comes from being honest, and realizing that many of our fears are actually just our egos and our monkey minds coming together to keep ourselves safe. Strength is when you accept every single part of yourself – the good, the bad, and the ugly. It is when you look your fears in the eye – and without judgment, acknowledge them, but put none of your power into them. True, unwavering strength comes when you do the things that make you feel uncomfortable. It occurs when your foundation is demolished, and you have no other choice but to be strong.

I have this strong belief that strength is a characteristic we are all born with, just like intuition. Like intuition, it is something that needs growth and development in order for it to manifest to its fullest potential. The choice to use it, is and will always be yours.

Loving from afar

As a Medium, I have my own language when it comes to Spirit Communication. Spirit will show me in my mind's eye, different visuals that allow me to know more about who they were here on Earth. I call these 'Calling Cards.'

One of my 'Calling Cards' is a brick wall. Literally, I see a massive brick wall. This is my indication that the

Spirit I am connecting with was stubborn, and hard headed. When talking to my client I would usually say "It was like talking to a brick wall."

This statement is usually accompanied with a sigh of relief or a "You have no idea," from my sitter.

Let's just say it like it is shall we? Some people are just pains in the ass. Some people are difficult. Some people are in our lives to remind us of what we don't want to be.

But just because they are a brick wall, doesn't mean there is less love in our hearts for them.

We use much of our time coming up with the things we want to say. We go over the sentences over and over again in our mind making sure that everything is precise and honest. We live in anxiety until we finally build up the courage to speak to the person.

We say our carefully constructed words with kindness and empathy; we feel our hearts racing, hands shaking, and egos trying to pull us back from speaking our truth.

After it's done, after the words are spoken, we expect a light bulb to go off. A sign. Anything to let us know our words were heard, our feelings are justified, and our hurt is something that can be healed.

And if we are lucky, everything ends up working out. And if we aren't, nothing changes.

You see in the eyes of the person you approached, that not one ounce of your truth was processed. There is not one sign that indicates the person feels remorse, or sorrow, or guilt, or understanding. There is nothing there to work with.

You end of up feeling defeated and confused. You wonder why you wasted so much of your time and effort into constructing your approach. You start to question yourself.

THIS IS WHERE YOU STOP.

DON'T GO ANY FURTHER.

Here is a #truthbomb you need to hear.

Some people will never get it. They will never be on your level. Just because YOUR consciousness has grown, does not mean theirs has or ever will. Just because you have decided to heal, doesn't mean they will heal along with you.

You are only in control of you.

Some people are lifelong soul connections.

Some people are here for a couple of seasons.

And some are just assholes.

The healing and growth never stops..

I have been sitting here at my desk for 20 minutes staring out a small window listening to the Fed Ex trucks and my neighbors' ATVs whisking down my street. My mind has been racing all day, my emotions have been all over the place. In just the last 12 hours I have felt angry, sad, disappointed, kind of okay, annoyed, tired, bored, and then kind of okay again. These days for me are occasional visitors, but none the less they still create a home within me from time to time.

There is this fucked up misconception in the spiritual community that to be a spiritual person, you need to be all high vibrations and love and light 100% of the time. That is just incorrect. I heard Brooke Castillo say once on her podcast that life is 50% good and 50% bad. And that simple statement was one of the most profound pieces of wisdom I have ever heard in my life. The human experience is filled with experiences to help with the evolution of one's soul.

And before you are a healer, before you are a coach, a spiritual teacher, a lightworker, a beacon of light, before you put all the labels under your name – you, my friend are a soul.

You need to experience it in order to create a space for others to heal themselves.

The spiritual community is growing at a rapid speed at this time. People are 'waking up' in droves, it is safe to say the shift has begun. Yet, I have to share what I have experienced because it is a virus that plaguing the community.

Spirituality can be used as the answer, but it can be also used as a band-aid. People flock to new age concepts such as manifestation, law of attraction, and twin flames not because their actual soul is drawn to it, but because it is an interesting distraction they use in order to avoid doing the actual work.

What is the work?

- Becoming aware of what triggers you? Start asking yourself "Why is this triggering me?" instead of becoming reactive.

- Become aware of your toxic tendencies
- What are your unhealed wounds?
- What haven't you forgiven whether it be forgiving someone else or yourself.
- What are your limiting beliefs?
- What are the main themes in your life, when it comes to hard lessons and healing (example – self worth, body image, money, relationships..)
- Where do you need to establish boundaries?
- Healing your inner child
- Forgiving your inner critic

I'm not going to lie, the work can get uncomfortable. The work can bring up emotions that you stored so well because you didn't like the way they felt the first time around. But you have to remember, you already felt it. You already have been through it. Think of this time as a review and not so much having to go through everything again.

Energy cannot be created or destroyed.

You don't have to go through the same thing others have endured. We all have our experiences, or own traumas, and our own journeys. But in order to forge a path for another, in order to be a beacon and to create a safe place for healing to occur, one must experience healing for themselves. I think of healing like the ocean. Powerful, beautiful, peaceful, turbulent, rough, dangerous.

CHAPTER SIX

ENERGY

'Everything is energy and that's all there is to it. Match the frequency to the reality you want and you cannot help but get that reality. It cannot be any other way. This is not philosophy. This is physics.'

— Albert Einstein

One of the most important things to understand is energy is everything. What allows us to distinguish between different things is the rate at which it vibrates. Everyone has their own frequency and vibration. Different thoughts create different vibrations. Our vibration is created by the thoughts we think, the actions we take, and the choices we make. In this chapter, we are going to learn fundamental tools to radically shift your own energy as well as give you the knowledge to discern when your energy is feeling off.

THE BIG THREE

When diving into both spiritual and personal growth, it is important to understand YOUR energy, but also energy as a whole. Many of our problems stem from a lack of knowledge of how to take care of our own energy, as well as how to properly protect ourselves.

Through my work, I have had the privilege to connect with many people from all different walks of life. Whether for a spiritual reading or for mentorship, I have come to find regardless of what kind of life you lead or what you do for a living, many of the problems that arise for us as individuals, come from our energy being disrupted.

Some of these problems or symptoms people may have are a lack of drive or focus, overwhelming anxiety, feeling sluggish or out of sorts, extreme exhaustion, and insomnia. All of these are symptoms that can be byproducts of your own energetic field

not being in balance. Now, don't get me wrong, sometimes life is a-son-of-a-bitch; we go through seasons of overwhelming chaos, upheaval, and growth, where your energy is not going to be at one hundred percent.

But many times our energy is off because we are holding onto energy that is not ours.

Have you ever felt irritated or aggravated without any reason?

Have you ever felt anxious without having anything that would cause anxiety? Have you ever had a long day where you were exhausted but then bedtime came and you couldn't fall asleep?

Have you ever had trouble focusing on a task or project?

All these things are examples of being ungrounded, not properly protected, or energetically cleansed. When it comes to energy, always come back to the big three:

GROUND – PROTECT – AND CLEAR.

GROUND

Grounding is a very popular term within the spiritual community. Grounding is the simple practice of connecting your energetic field to the Earth's energetic field. One of the biggest issues society, as a whole, has today is a lack of connection to Earth. So many of both our mental and physical ailments stem from a lack of Earth energy within our own energy field. This can leave us feeling lightheaded, disconnected, anxious, irritable, and whole mess of other things.

There are many ways to ground your energy with the most simple being: envisioning roots growing from the bottom of your feet and making their way down to the center of the Earth. Grounding is an essential step you must take if your intention is to deepen your connection to source and live a peaceful and balanced life.

EARTH CONNECTION EXERCISE:

Items needed:

Black tourmaline

Carnelian

Smoky Quartz

Onyx

Selenite

A playlist of your favorite meditation music, tribal music, shamanic drumming.

(Please note, all of these items are optional, they are simply shared to add to your experience.)

Find a quiet, comfortable place outside, where you will not be disturbed and you will be able to lie comfortably for at least 30 minutes. Once you have found your sanctuary, sit in the pretzel style position with your palms facing up against your knees. Close your eyes and take five deep breaths. With every inhale envision yourself taking in the calming, powerful energy of Mother Earth bringing it into your lungs and body, and with every exhale envision yourself releasing and getting rid of any energy not serving your highest and greatest good.

Invoke Gaia to come and merge her energy with yours by stating out loud or in your mind,

'Divine Mother Gaia,

I call upon thee,

I call upon your healing, your light, and your power.

I ask to merge with your energy at this time.

Allow me to be an extension of you,

Allow me to feel your energy within my own.

I invite you Sacred Mother,

To co-create with me at this time.'

Once the invitation has been spoken, gather any crystals you have chosen, and your music. Intuitively lay the crystals upon your body and start your playlist. Tune into the subtle energy of the Earth's aura, and her pulse. Attune your natural pulse to the one of Gaia's.

Allow Gaia to heal you. Allow her to show you her ability to guide you, teach you, and honor you. Let the experience and connection be yours and yours alone.

PROTECT

This part of the process is pretty self-explanatory. The act of energetic protection is simply protecting your own energetic field and space from outside forces. These forces can be both from the physical and spiritual planes.

We live in a universe of duality, which means both positive and negative energies exist. There is black and white, left and right, up and down. The same goes for good and bad. Spiritual protection has become a very controversial topic within the spiritual community. Many mediums, psychics, and healers hold the belief there is nothing to protect ourselves against when it comes to the spiritual world. Yet, there are others who are adamant about protecting one's energy and space. Being the Aquarius I am, and being open to all possibilities and viewpoints, I am going to share my insight on this subject.

Whether you believe we should protect ourselves or not, there is not one person on this Earth or in Spirit form who can tell us everything about the Spirit World. Would you tell someone what clothes to pack on their trip to Alaska if you haven't actually visited? When you are a Psychic Medium, you have the ability to be a channel or an operator, if you will, with someone who has crossed over. You receive impressions and information through your psychic senses. You don't go on a day trip to the Spirit World. The truth is, we don't know enough about Spirit or the Spirit World to tell people they shouldn't protect their energy and space when we are only basing our opinion on our own experience.

Now, minus the spiritual aspect of protection, there are forces within the physical world that aren't necessarily of the highest vibration that can have a negative effect on us. Things like psychic attacks, energy vampires, stagnant negative energy... these things are real and depending on how open we are and how powerful the force is, can really have a negative effect on us. Whether you believe you need an extra layer of protection or not, I simply ask you at least try the exercises and techniques I share with you in this book for at least a week and see if you feel a difference within your own energy.

To make grounding and protection simple, I start every day with a very basic grounding and protection meditation before I get out of bed. Living a more spiritual based life shouldn't be hard, it should be easy and feel natural. If you'd like to listen to my guided grounding and protection meditation for free, you can do so on my YouTube channel.

PROTECTION EXERCISE:

Close your eyes and start tuning into the natural rhythm of your breathing. Bring your attention to the top of your head, and in your mind call upon

Archangel Michael, and ask him to protect you in his white and gold light. Envision this powerful white and gold light cascading down your entire body until it reached the bottom of your feet. Expand this light outward by three feet. In your mind, thank Archangel Michael for his protection.

CLEARING

Have you ever cleaned your home from top to bottom with the faint smell of Pine Sol or Fabuloso, proud of your hard work, to then wake up the next morning and have it turn completely back in shambles? Yeah, me too. Clearing one's energy is just as important as cleaning one's home.

Depending on what your lifestyle looks like, we are constantly being bombarded with energy that is not ours, and sometimes these energies can leave us feeling irritable, drained, and sometimes down right exhausted. When I do readings, I can't tell you how many times my clients problems stemmed from them not clearing their energy and space, and essentially having a collection of unwanted, negative energy that isn't even theirs, around them!

A personal story I'd like to share. I once had a reading with a lovely woman who was struggling with random spurts of anger and anxiety. She worked at a bank, as a teller, with a small group of people and was constantly coming into contact with customers as well as her co-workers. A new assistant manager started about six weeks prior to her reading with me and she noticed her energetic shift started to occur around that time. She complained of random spurts of anxiety with no reasoning behind it. She would become aggressive and frustrated over things she wouldn't normally get upset over, and she was struggling 3-4 nights a week with reoccurring insomnia.

She told me how her new assistant manager was very highly strung, and wasn't a good fit for the position. I told her how to ground and protect her energy properly, as well as to invest in selenite and black tourmaline and keep them around her workplace. She agreed and did what I said. A week later she emailed me letting me know what I suggested was working to an extent, but that she would still feel anxious and deal with insomnia at night time. At this point, I asked my guides for some guidance and I saw a large laundry basket in my mind's eye. I wasn't quite sure where this piece of information was going to take me, but I responded to her email asking her if she has her laundry basket that holds her dirty clothes and the energy from the day in her bedroom. She said yes, and after that, everything started to make perfect sense. You see, energy cannot be created or destroyed. My client's clothes were holding the energy she experienced throughout her work day. Every interaction, every transaction, every conversation was being stored within the fibers of her clothes which she then left in an open laundry basket in her bedroom. She was doing a great job at grounding and protecting her energy but she was essentially coming home and bringing the energy of the day with her and leaving it in a pile at the side of her room. Once I pointed this out, she agreed this made a lot of sense, and found another place to store her dirty laundry. Since this change, she hasn't had any issues.

I wanted to share this story with you because it is a great example of how powerful energy can be as well as how easy it is to be effected by energy that is not ours. As the logical human beings we are, we have this overwhelming need to justify and rationalize, to pinpoint and to make sense of. When diving into your Spiritual Path, the most important thing to remember is the logical mind is here to keep us human. It is here to keep us safe, and to help us try to understand the unexplainable. The intention of this book isn't to help you make sense of every spiritual synchronicity and every vivid dream and experience you have in meditation. The intention of this book is to show you that being a Mystic, being intuitive, is your natural state of being.

TAKING INVENTORY

This is an exercise

I learned a while back from one of my teachers, and I have kept it in my back pocket ever since.

This is a great exercise anytime you just need to come back into your body, check in with yourself, or before doing any spiritual work.

Begin the exercise by finding a quiet comfortable place where you will not be disturbed for about ten minutes or so. Sit with your feet firmly planted on the ground and close your eyes. Allow yourself to focus on the natural rhythm of your breath and begin to bring yourself to a state where your mind becomes quiet. Once you have reached this state, tune into your physical energy field. Notice any tension in your physical body, any sensations that are present at this time. Take note of them. We are coming into this exercise without any judgment. We are simply taking note of what is present within our personal energy at this time. Once you have fully scanned your entire physical body, start taking note of what emotions are currently present for you at this time. Once you have finished with this step, bring your attention to your mental body. What thoughts are currently in your conscious mind? What thoughts are spending the most time in your mind and energy. Once you have tapped into your physical, emotional, and mental bodies, you can bring yourself back into the present moment.

CLEANSE AND PURIFICATION BATH SPELL:

Items Needed:

1 Cup Sea Salt

1 Cup Epsom Salt

½ cup baking soda

1 Lemon cut into 7 round pieces

Selenite Wand

Begin this process by filling your bath with warm water, or at a comfortable temperature for you. Add the Sea Salt, Epsom Salt, and baking soda. The 7 pieces of lemon symbolize each of your major chakras. One at a time, throw a cut slice of lemon into the bath while stating out loud the chakra it represents. (The 7 Major Chakras are Root, Sacral, Solar Plexus, Heart, Throat, Brow, and Crown.) Once all of the ingredients are added to the bath, begin the taking inventory exercise found in the previous section. Take note of how your energy feels at this exact moment.

If you are feeling run down, tired, fatigued, disconnected – take the selenite wand and starting at your feet slowly bring the wand up your entire body while you envision the energy within you being balanced out.

If you are feeling flighty, spaced out, unable to concentrate. Start with the selenite wand at the top of your head and begin making its way down your entire body envisioning your energy being balanced out and distributed evenly throughout your whole body.

If you don't feel either way, and just want to clear your auric field, close your eyes and call upon your guides to help you intuitively sweep your energy, getting rid of any energy not serving your highest and greatest good.

Once this exercise is completed, you may enter the bath. Allow yourself to soak for at least 30 minutes without taking a shower afterwards. We want the salts to work their magic even after your time in the bath is completed.

CHAPTER SEVEN

SURRENDER

The word surrender brings a wave of emotions with it. I talk about surrendering a lot, especially in my mediumship development circles. One of the more enjoyable parts of my job is when I announce there will be breakout rooms (where you are put in a private room with someone else and you have to give each other readings) and nearly every face on the screen changes to either disbelief, shock, or resting bitch face, and they throw me a quick bird (with love, of course). Why does this happen? Why do jaws drop, eyes grow big, and anxiety runs high every time my clients are faced with having to do a mediumship reading? Because in order to be a medium, one must not only learn, but master the art of surrender.

Mediumship is the energetic connection between a soul who has passed, onto the medium. The medium opens themselves up and receives evidence from Sprit that confirms who they were in their most recent past life. I use this example because it is one I know well, and one label that requires a lot of surrendering.

When it comes to being a medium, you are the messenger not the storyteller.

You are simply the tube. The channel. The telephone operator.

Now, even if you are not a medium and you have no intention of becoming one, this chapter will still be extremely beneficial to you. The teaching and the tools in this chapter are for everyone, and if you are someone who is sitting there reading this with that tightness in your chest, and resistance to turn to the next page, this chapter is DEFINITELY for you.

If you are reading this book because you want to transform your life,

If you are reading this book because you want to learn to trust your inner voice,

If you are reading this book because you want to step into your next level you with Spirit as your ally,

You need to first learn how to surrender.

I don't know one person who is comfortable with the idea of giving all their 'power' away to something they have no control over. You need give yourself some grace; you need to allow yourself patience and time. This is not a destination, it's a journey, an intricately woven process. Surrender is the key to true power, a power that resides in every one of us. A power far greater than one can imagine. You hold the magic of the night sky within you. You hold the wisdom of a thousand masters within you. You hold the power of all of creation within you. You hold the power of magnificent abundance and unconditional love within you. But before you access the magic, you must learn to surrender to it.

EXERCISE

Grab your journal or a piece of paper and pen. Make eight boxes and label them: Fun & Recreation, Career, Money, Personal Growth, Spiritual Growth, Relationships, Environment, and Health. Go through all the problems you are facing in each category and write them in the boxes. Once you go through all of them, how many of the problems that you are currently facing have to do with your lack of surrender? Go ahead and cross those things out, if that is the case.

How many of your problems were you able to cross out? Some? Most? All of them? Sometimes all it takes is a different perspective in order to see things more clearly. Go through this exercise any time you feel resistance in your life.

Loosen the reins

If you were to have met me before I started developing my mediumship, you would have met a mom with no makeup, hair in a messy bun, black leggings, an oversized graphic tee and $12 fake Uggs from Primark, slowly roaming the halls of Target with a Starbucks, looking at all the shit she doesn't need, but throwing it in her cart anyway.

You would have met a 30 something year old downing Mexican restaurant salsa like it's soup, and not able to keep a white shirt clean. If you met me before my awakening (and now), you would meet a mom who was a personal snack bitch who says "Yes" to every new snack request, because that is just who I am. I consider myself many things, but being Type A was never one of them, until I embarked on the path of mediumship.

Mediumship requires a level of surrender many, if not most, people are not comfortable with. It requires a level of faith most people do not have. The first two years of my path into mediumship, my rational self, the one who pays the bills, gets the kids on the bus and goes grocery shopping, struggled immensely with surrendering. I joined free Facebook groups for psychic and mediumship development and would practice giving readings as much as my energy would allow. I would keep tabs on my accurate and not accurate hits. As I continued to hone in on my development, I had a lady private message me whom I read (for free) and she told me that her son had been gone for seven years and she had been to many mediums around the UK, and none of the readings came close to mine. She told me how well I brought the essence of her son through and asked for my business information. I told her I didn't have a business yet and I was still developing. She messaged me back with a laughing crying face emoji and then said,

"Hunni, you are developed, you should be getting paid for the healing you bring."

I wish she knew what a positive impact she had on me and my mediumship journey. Hearing encouraging words from a kind stranger really is some of the best medicine.

After she said that, I went to my binder where I kept tallies of my 'hits' and decided to count them up. Including her reading, I had 72 accurate readings and 6 not accurate readings. I was speechless. I was so busy trying to prove myself wrong, I didn't give myself credit for all the things I did right. The entire time I was collecting these tallies, I was fighting a battle within myself. With every reading where my sitter was happy and blown away with what came through, my inner bitch was saying things like. "This can just be a coincidence," or "You should have gotten a name or better evidence."

There was healing happening for the Spirit and for the sitter, but I was fighting a lonely battle within myself. I refused to surrender. I refused to wave a white flag and truly trust the process. I needed more evidence, BETTER evidence, no reading was enough for ME.

I can't tell you the exact moment it happened. There wasn't any spark of inspiration or divine download that changed the trajectory as far as my mediumship is concerned. I honestly just think my soul got tired of fighting. I slowly started to step back from the stories

I was telling myself and began leaning into love. I began to realize my own insecurities were dimming my light. I was my own worst enemy.

If you take anything away from this chapter, please have it be this. Nobody is as hard on you as you are. Nobody is judging you as much as you are judging yourself. You can have high standards and still be kind and gentle to yourself. You can be a work of progress and a masterpiece at the same time. You can be the teacher and the student. It doesn't have to be perfect, you just have to try your best.

Something that really helped me in the surrender process, whether it was for mediumship, or doing the plank position, or stepping into cold water – before stepping into something that required me to surrender, I would take a deep breath and look at myself in the mirror and say out loud "Erica, for [insert number here] minutes, you can surrender. You can do anything."

Whether we like it or not, surrendering is a part of the human experience. It is something that every single person has to overcome at least once in their life. When I think of surrender I see the visual of strong hands holding onto a rope. The muscles tense and the knuckles bloody. You can sense the agony in the person who is holding on. The pain is there, it is real and raw and tangible, yet if they were to just surrender and let go, the excruciating pain would be gone. The battle would be over. Peace will take the place of pain. That is the power of surrender.

There are many things you have the power to control, but you don't have the power to control everything. In all honesty, would you want that? Would you want that burden of having to control everything? I know I wouldn't. So why do we still allow things outside of our control to create discomfort in our reality? Why are the greatest battles we fight within ourselves, and always ones that require us to surrender to what is?

The reason there is so much fear around the concept of surrender is because it feels like we are giving away our power when, in fact, we gain so much more when we do surrender. We create stories around it that instil fear and make us totally paralyzed from the concept. Most of our problems stem from a lack of surrender. When we learn to surrender to the things that we have no control over, life, as we know it, gets better.

When I was a kid, my family would vacation every summer in Rhode Island. We would spend our days at the beach and my cousin Sam and I would be in the water. We would always find ourselves in that awkward spot right before the undertow but where the waves would crash and take us down. We would try so hard to run away from the crashing of the waves, but we would always find ourselves completely wiped out by them unable to see because our hair was in the way of our eyes and our crotches were filled with sand. We continued the cycle for many years until one year, we found the courage to not run away from the wave, but instead, dive into it. We found ourselves being able to flow with the ocean rather than fight it.

What is the point in fighting if on the other side of that battle is peace?

Wherever you are,

You are safe.

Whatever is outside of your control,

You are safe.

Whatever pain is present,

You are safe.

Whatever is making you feel disconnected from source is just a layer that is put upon by one's self.

You are never disconnected from source.

You are never far away from love.

If you cannot see it,

Close your eyes.

If you cannot feel it,

Close your eyes.

If you cannot hear it,

Close your eyes.

If you cannot believe it,

Close your eyes.

You are never far away from love.

You are never far away from the light.

We guide you through your thoughts and feelings,

We whisper words of encouragement in your ear.

We are always beside you,

We never lead you astray.

We hold you when you cry,

We watch you when you grow,

We applaud you when you become.

You are never alone.

You are never too far away.

You are always love.

Archangel Michael

Of all the deities, archangels, and ascended masters I have ever learned about, worked with, or experienced, Archangel Michael has been the most influential and powerful force within my life. He has been a constant, a trusted advisor, my ultimate guardian and protector. Archangel Michael is one of the two archangels who appeared in the Bible and has gained a reputation here on Earth as 'The Protector.'

I wish I could put into words the power Archangel Michael has to protect, but I don't believe I would be able to do him any justice. Instead, I'd like to share a personal experience I had while calling upon him.

In 2018, the area in which I live (NY/CT area), got hit with a microburst. A microburst is essentially four tornadoes in one, aka, a total shit show. I was at home with my 6 year and 4 year old at this time, and my husband was at his mother's house helping her move furniture, before he made his way back home. We were aware there was a possible hurricane touching down but being on the East Coast, this wasn't anything new. I could see from the front window the storm was coming close when I got a frantic phone call from my husband. He told me he had just witnessed two large trees come down on his mother's front yard with one of them crossing over onto the street. He told me to take the kids and the pets downstairs to the basement immediately as the tornado was making its way towards our town next.

As quickly as I could, I grabbed the kids, the dog, and the cat and locked ourselves in our basement. As I gathered everyone to the same room, I intuitively dropped to my knees in prayer position, and prayed to Archangel Michael. I don't remember what I said exactly, but I knew I asked him to protect my family and my property. We sat downstairs in our dark basement for what felt like forever until the winds and rain subsided.

I went outside to assess the damage to find the neighborhood in utter devastation. Trees on houses, neighbor's cars, electrical wires everywhere. Never in my life did I think I would see something as devastating as this with my own eyes. As I was walking around my own property I noticed a couple of downed branches we would be able to dispose of easily but nothing that affected the house or my vehicle. All my neighbors had much more extensive damage on their properties and cars. I stood in my front yard with my mouth wide open completely blown away by what had just transpired and how my prayer to Archangel Michael protected my family and my home.

It took the town and the cleanup crew two days to clear the roads for my husband to be able to come home. I didn't tell him about praying to Archangel Michael before the storm hit. To be honest, I wasn't quite sure he would believe the miracle we were just part of. When he finally was able to make his way home, he did the same walk around inspection of the house I did two days prior. We met each other in front of the house. He stood there scratching his head and looking bewildered.

I asked him, "What's wrong?" and he told me from where the large branches landed on our property, it looked as if our house and my car were in some sort of "protective bubble". I humbly smiled when he said that and agreed with him.

I told him about my prayer to Archangel Michael down in the basement, and he answered with,

"Well, it looks like it worked!"

I never told anyone besides my husband about this story until my good friend had a very similar experience back in March of 2020. She lives in Georgia and was woken up in the middle of the night by a tornado warning on her phone. She gathered her family and went into a closet on the lowest floor of her house. As her family gathered close inside the closet, her nine year old son intuitively started praying out loud to Archangel Michael. Both she and her son were completely unaware of my experience two years prior. Like any natural disaster, the tornado that touched down in her area brought immense tragedy and devastation to her town. People lost their homes, and many were out of power and internet service for up to five weeks. Yet, her property had minimal damage.

Both these stories combined truly shows the powerful protection Archangel Michael instills upon us when we ask. I truly believe if we really knew how much help we really do receive from the other side, whether it is from Archangel Michael or from our own spirit guides, we would never feel unsafe. We would never question, and we would never argue there is something far greater than what we see with our eyes. In the next section, I am going to share with you one of my favorite prayers to bring powerful results. I recited this prayer every Tuesday for nine consecutive weeks. I also lit a seven day candle prior to each time I prayed, to honor Archangel Michael as he helped me in my struggle with truly surrendering.

Although this is a powerful method to help you surrender, you can use this prayer for anything with which you would like help or assistance. Maybe it is heartbreak, emotional healing, grieving, whatever it is Archangel Michael can help you and can bring miraculous miracles along with him.

THE PRAYER:

"St. Michael, I resort to your protection and in my faith offer this light {a candle} which shall burn every Tuesday.

Comfort me in difficulties and the lodging in the house of our savior, intercede for me and my family that we will be able to hold God close to our hearts and be provided for in all of our necessities. I beseech you to have infinite pity in regard to the favors that I ask of you (name them) that I may be able to overcome all difficulties as you did the dragon at your feet."

Say 3 'Hail Marys'

"Hail Mary, full of grace, the Lord is with thee. Blessed are thou amongst women and blessed is the fruit of thy womb, Jesus.

Holy Mary, Mother of God, pray for us sinners now until the hour of our death. Amen"

Say 3 'Our Fathers'

Our Father, who art in heaven, hallowed be thy name. Thy kingdom come, thy will be done on earth as it is in heaven. Give us this day our daily bread and forgive us of our trespasses as we forgive those who trespass against us. Lead us not into temptation but deliver us from evil. For thine is the kingdom, and the power, and the glory, forever and ever, amen."

Say 3 'Glory Bes'

Glory be to the Father and to the Son and to the Holy Spirit as it was in the beginning is now and ever shall be world without end. Amen."

Finding Faith

Faith is not something we find. It is not something that comes after the storm has passed, or when a miracle unravels itself in front of us. Faith is something that is a part of us. Like intuition, we come into this Earth with it.

Faith is not something we must find, it is something we must remember.

Little by little, it drifts away. It becomes cloudy. It becomes lost in the trenches and eventually, we can lose it. But it hasn't gone anywhere. It's never left us. Our faith doesn't decide to walk out the door one day never to be seen again, Your faith has been there for you. It has been there in your darkest moments, it has been there at rock bottom, and it has been there when you didn't believe it to be. Faith is the only thing left when you have nothing else.

Whatever religious or spiritual background you come from, no matter what god or deity you worship or pray to, it all comes down to faith.

Whether you have been walking the spiritual path for years or have just started to open up to your own spirituality and connection, please know this:

Your spiritual path is yours. It has always been and always will be. You get to decide what works for you. You get to choose the practices, the rituals, and the beliefs that allow you to feel connected to your soul and to be your most authentic self.

You get to try things on, and take things off.

You get to style your spirituality as you see fit.

So whether that is dancing naked in the woods under a full moon, meditating in a buddhist monastery, or praying to Christ in Church, you are the only person that gets to decide what shape your faith comes in.

Become the eternal student. Try different things. Experience what spirituality and life has to offer. There is no hurry to figure out what your faith looks like, as long as you have faith in yourself in the meantime.

CHAPTER EIGHT

GODDESS

She is the phoenix rising from the ashes,

She is the wave crashing over cliffs,

Her power is silent and still,

Her voice is strong and determined.

She walks with a broken and open heart.

Her mind, a sponge,

And her womb holds the power of all creation.

She is wise.

She is compassionate.

She is an unstoppable force.

She searches far and wide for the answers,

Sitting humbly at the feet of wisest mentors and teachers,

To search for the answers that were within her all along.

She is a healer, a mystic, a force to be reckoned with.

She is humble and kind,

Wild and free.

She is the maiden, mother, and the crone.

She is both the witch and the warrior.

She finds solace in nature,

And healing in silence.

She stands alone and stands for all.

She leads herself through the darkest times,

Blind and afraid,

Only to realize at the end, she was the light.

When we think of The Goddess, we will often paint a picture in our minds of some beautiful mysterious being wrapped in gold and being carried down a marble staircase by humble servants. We will picture Greek Goddesses with flowing white dresses drinking wine and eating grapes while cherubs play harps in the background. Our human mind will picture these scenarios because it wants to try to make sense of it. It wants to put this unpalatable, powerful force in some sort of box so our rational human brains can comprehend The Goddess.

The Goddess is the powerful force that resides within your womb.

It is the innate beauty of your soul.

It is the all-knowing and ever learning part of yourself.

It is the connection to all creation.

It is the power that creates worlds.

It is your connection to Mother Earth.

It is your divine oneness to every woman.

The Goddess is not something you have to seek outside yourself. She is already within you. All you must do is create space for her to rise. Your Goddess seeks solitude in nature. She desires comfort, and nourishment, from all that Mother Earth gives us. She will be found in the darkest times when one must find the strength to rise above. She shows herself at your most confident, as well as your most vulnerable.

She thrives when one rises with other goddesses, and when one listens to the whispers of one's soul. She enjoys being surrounded by beauty, but will heal herself in the darkest and ugliest of places. She is the gentle force one feels when it is time to take a leap of faith. She is a self-healer, a warrior, and a fighter.

She honors the cycle of the moon,

And evolves like the changing of seasons.

Her compassion is undeniable,

Yet her love for self comes before anything else.

She knows who she is,

And what she stands for.

"You must understand, they fear you. There is nothing scarier in their minds than a girl who knows the power of her flames."

-Nikita Gill

I looked at myself in the mirror, and all I could do was make a snarl and reminisce about the times I actually gave a shit about what I looked like. Memories of my early twenties flashed before my eyes when I would spend my Thursday lunch break at Forever 21 searching through the racks to find the cutest $24.99 dress to wear on my Friday night out on the town. I'd schedule in at least 60 minutes to get ready which included a shower and perfecting my makeup in front of my mom's makeup mirror. I would have *Spice Girls* playing in the background, or if I was feeling extra emo that day, *Taking Back Sunday* or *Brand New* would be the soundtracks of choice.

Life was easier back then... When my outfit on a Friday night and what eyeliner color would match my Forever 21 dress were my biggest problems. There is this thing that happens between the time you are a 20 something year old female with not a care in the world, to when you become a 30 something year old mother. In your mind, you expect the change. You know it is bound to happen. A marriage, children, a mortgage... life. But all these life altering events always seems to happen when you are too busy with other things. You have the facebook photos to prove that you have grown up, got engaged, bought the house, had the baby, and yet you will still find yourself looking back, wondering when did life happen?

When did the girl that used to sneak in her own liquor to the bar, make friends with every person in line for the girls bathroom, watched *Gossip Girl* and *One Tree Hill* religiously, turn into a grown up?

Life is a collection of seasons that all somehow blend together. There are going to be seasons of change, and of heartbreak. There will be seasons of adventure, and contemplation. There are going to be seasons where you are going to want to fast forward it, and seasons that you will never want to leave. Whatever season you are in, know this: there is always something to take from it.

Trust the process & trust yourself.

Remember the power you have.

Remember the love in your heart & the lessons you have already passed.

When you find yourself discouraged because the path ahead looks like a long one, remember to take a peek in back of you to see how far you have already come.

Womb Power Ritual

This powerful ritual is one I used often to write this book. It is extremely powerful when you are wanting to express yourself creatively with the Universe and your goddess as your co-captain. This ritual is also good for connecting to your natural sexual nature.

Items Needed

Orange candle (white will work as well)

Matches/lighter

Optional

Dress the candle with an attraction oil and herbs like catnip, rose, and jasmine, or allow your intuition to guide you to the herbs your womb needs at this time.

Sit in an upright position. Bring the orange candle close your womb (about 2-3 inches below your belly button). Start by envisioning your womb as an unlit fireplace or fire pit. While holding the candle, infuse your intentions into the candle by visualizing what it is you are trying to manifest. If you are wanting to use this ritual to write a book, or create a program, or start a project, envision the outcome or the process. Set the intention for the inspiration to flow through you in a natural and easy way. If you are using this ritual to experience more pleasure, envision the outcome of what that looks like for you.

Once you feel your intentions are strong and fully infused within the candle, state out loud,

"With this, I co-create with my womb, with this I connect to my Goddess. With this I am the creator."

Light the candle and bring it as close as you can to your sacral chakra without burning yourself of course, and envision the flame of the candle lighting the fire in your womb. State out loud,

"I am the channel, I am The Goddess, I am the creator." Place your candle on your altar or in a safe place. You are now open and ready to create!!

MEET YOUR GODDESS MEDITATION

Find a quiet comfortable place where you will not be disturbed. For this meditation, I like to light a tea light candle with the intention of inviting my guides and my Goddess in. Once the tea light is lit, go ahead and close your eyes. Start tuning into the natural rhythm of your breath. Allow your inhales to become naturally deeper, and your exhales longer. Take some time to truly get into that calm and quiet place in your own mind. In your mind's eye, envision a door in front on you. Start making your way to the door. As you approach the door, allow your hand to reach for the knob and open the door. There before you will stand the most beautiful, powerful, magnetic Goddess you have ever encountered. Take note of what she is wearing, her face, her hair, and how you feel in her presence. As you observe, she holds out her hands for you to come closer. Begin making your way to her and reach out to connect your hand with hers. Allow yourself to be fully immersed in this reconnection to her, to your Goddess. Here you can ask her any questions, or just begin to embody her energy. Stay with her as long as you wish. When you feel it is time to part ways, you can wish her well, and begin to make your way back to the door, back to the present, and back into your body. Feel free to write about your experience or any messages that came through for you.

Letting her work through you

She awakens in the middle of the night,

As the rays of the harvest moon peek through the sides of the blinds in her bedroom.

She lays restless, listening to the humming of the air conditioning unit beside her.

"Come back in the morning," she speaks.

Knowing this is the call of the Dark Goddess.

"Can you let me sleep? I promise I will let you write through me in the morning."

She closes her eyes once more in hopes to find peace, yet the restlessness grows stronger, the yearning to share what is brewing inside her continues to evolve, keeping her mind awake.

Thirty minutes pass and she finally surrenders.

"Okay, FINE!" she mumbles.

The Dark Goddess grins as she claims her victory.

As the woman grabs her computer and begins to make her way down the hallway, she knows she is a servant to the Dark Goddess. As frustrated as she is at the unshakable insomnia her body is experiencing at this moment, she knows there is no rest for those who honor the shadow self, the dark goddess.

As she finds herself at 2:31am tip-toeing silently through her house with her laptop in tow, she catches a glimpse of the powerful force in the sky that has awakened her.

The light of the moon is so bright, it can be mistaken for sunrise. And yet, as the world sleeps around her, she is awake, tormented by the words wanting to be birthed in the rays of the harvest moon.

Although these visitations from the goddess are not frequent, she knows them all too well.

She knows that when she calls, there is no bargaining, or fighting it.

There is no turning your cheek or falling back to sleep.

The Goddess shows up when she wants, and she does not take no for an answer.

This relationship between the woman and the Dark Goddess has been one of mentor and student, friend and foe, mother and child. It has been the one relationship in the woman's life that has pushed her further than she ever thought possible.

This relationship has brought more tears than any other connection she has ever experienced in her 34 years on this Earth.

It is the relationship that makes her the most uncomfortable, the most lost, the most scared, the most disconnected to the outer realms of reality.

This relationship between the woman and the Dark Goddess was birthed in a war zone. With the casualties being each of the excuses and stories the woman has carefully curated through the years that have kept her safe. You see, the Dark Goddess sees right through her. She is not here to console or hold your hand as you cry and play the victim. She is here to ignite the flames and rip the stories from your grip and throw them into the fire as you whimper with your head laying in your hands collecting the tears.

She does not console, she demands.

She does not nourish, she depletes.

She does not honor, she teaches.

She does not cherish, she pushes.

She does not create, she destroys.

Those who are well versed in her teachings, are the women who rise from the ashes. They are the ones with resilient spirits, with unbreakable hearts. They are the ones who come out on the other side, every single time, in spite of the challenges and hardships they face.

They are the warriors,

The lighthouses,

The rebels.

They are the visionaries,

The humanitarians,

And the revolutionaries.

They are the leaders,

The CEOS,

And the story tellers.

Through their work with goddess they do not falter in the face of fear, they welcome it.

They honor their healing,

Are aware of their growth,

And choose their battles wisely.

They report within when life becomes heavy.

They find the answers they seek within the silence and darkness.

CHAPTER NINE

SPIRIT

When I was six years old, I was sledding at my grandparent's house in upstate New York. It was mid-January and there was at least a fresh foot of powdery white snow with a glisten of ice on top of it. It was the perfect combination for prime sledding. My grandmother and I started to get into the big blow up tube on the top of the hill and as we made our way down the hill, the last thing I remember was thinking to myself,

'Whoa we're going really fast.'

The next thing I remember was my grandmother picking me up by my armpits and looking down at the white snow and seeing bright red blood everywhere in front of me. We made our way back to the house where my grandparents cleaned me up and my grandfather was wiping my forehead with a wet washcloth as he stated,

"Jesus Christ, you can see her skull."

My grandmother was pacing back and forth in the background, calling my parents on a phone that still had a cord. I was screaming bloody murder (literally) and my grandfather was infatuated with the fact that he could see his six year old granddaughter's skull. It was like a scene from a *National Lampoon* Movie.

The strangest thing about this was that even though all the blood scared the shit out of me, I didn't actually feel pain. I don't remember feeling the intense pain of my head initially hitting the rock. I don't remember feeling any throbbing or discomfort in my forehead. It was like for the 30 seconds when the crash happened, I was put in a bubble that kept me safe from the world. I ended up getting 17 stitches in my forehead that day, and a scar that would last a lifetime.

Life went back to normal rather quickly, and the story behind my scar became a distant memory. It wasn't until I started developing my intuitive and mediumship abilities this distant memory resurfaced. One day I was going into a deep meditation with the intention of wanting to connect with my spirit guides. I asked my main guide to show me a memory in my life where he was present. The picture of the white covered hill quickly flashed in my mind's eye. The whole event came back to me so quickly and clearly. I watched myself as a young child on the tube with my grandma. I watched as we lost control of the sled and I ended up catapulting head on into a large rock that was hidden by the thick layer of snow. It was in that moment I realized this event could have left me paralyzed, or with a traumatic brain injury. Yet, all that came from this was 17 stitches.

It is in those moments when unquestionable miracles occur that Spirit steps in. It is in those moments where we cannot justify or rationalize what has come to be.

If you knew how intertwined Spirit is with your life, you would never question the existence of something far greater.

It is the undeniable invisible force that guides us through our darkest moments and happiest memories. It is the knowing of a calm and loving presence when we feel most alone. Whether it is your own spirit guides, passed loved ones, or ascended masters, Spirit is always willing and able to serve.

Now, before I go any further, I am well aware there might be some skeptics or people [like myself] who like tangible proof or validation when it comes to anything esoteric. Our minds are programed that way. We receive intuition and universal inspiration through the right hemisphere of our brain, but then, this piece of information will quickly makes its way to the left hemisphere which is our analytical and rational side. I can't tell you how many times I worked with someone and they got an initial psychic/intuitive hit and then went on to say,

"I don't know if this makes any sense."

Or, "I am probably making this up but..."

We are naturally programmed to question, to analyze, and to try to make sense of things. It is just how we humans are. It is as natural as breathing or chewing or blinking. And unfortunately, there is no way around this. The only thing we can do is to be aware of the natural conditions with which we are faced.

Spirit exists; it is as real as the air we breathe. Past lives and reincarnation is real. Life after death is real. Angels and Spirit Guides are real. We all know this as fact at the soul level. Yet at the human level, we are put into a physical body that is hardwired to rationalize and dumb down everything we receive from source. We are naturally programmed to question our intuition and to take on the beliefs of others which makes having unquestionable faith in one's own Spirituality really fucking hard. But you can do hard things.

The exercises I share in this chapter are made to help you attune to and experience the subtle touch of Spirit. Your job throughout this process is to not question it. Don't judge the experience or what comes through, just be present and be open to anything that happens. Remember, your soul already knows it to be true; you just have to get your muggle self out of the way.

MEET YOUR SPIRIT GUIDES

Please note: There are many different ways and meditations available that will allow you to connect with your spirit guides and angels. I like to incorporate both an easy ritual as well as meditation as I feel it strengthens your intention and shows your guides and the Universe you mean business.

ITEMS NEEDED:

White Tea Light Candle

Matches/Lighter

Start by holding the tea light candle in your hands. Close your eyes and begin holding the intention of wanting to meet and connect with your Spirit Guides. Envision a powerful stream of energy starting from your heart making its way up to your shoulders and then down your arms and into your hands. Envision this energetic stream being infused into the tea light candle. Once you feel your intentions are infused into the candle, go ahead and light it. Place the candle in front of you and begin to close your eyes once again. Start tuning into the natural rhythm of your breath. Bring your awareness to the bottom of your feet where you will envision roots making their way down all the layers of Mother Earth. Allow the energy of Mother Earth to center and ground you. Once your roots are established, envision yourself being encompassed by a giant bubble of white and gold light. You are now grounded and protected. In your mind's eye, envision a door in front you. Behind this door you will meet your spirit guides. Start bringing yourself closer to the door and once you are ready, open the door. You will find yourself in your own inner sanctuary. This can be a crystal cave, a garden, a castle – it is completely yours.

ATTUNE WITH THE SPIRIT OF NATURE

Find a place in nature that is calm, inviting, and free from other people. I have found doing this exercise with a quartz crystal helps enhance the subtle energies of nature. Go ahead and get yourself into a comfortable position either holding the quartz crystal or placing it somewhere close to you. Begin by closing your eyes and focusing on your natural breathing rhythm. Continue to focus on your breath until you find your mind still from any thoughts or distractions. Once you reach this place of stillness, gently bring your awareness to the surrounding area. Tune into the sounds and subtle vibrations that are present. The key to this exercise isn't to observe nature, but rather to realize you are a part of it. After connecting with the Spirit of Nature, I always like to express a moment of gratitude.

STAIRCASE TO HEAVEN

This is an exercise I learned from one of my Mediumship Teachers, Janet Nohavec, and it always brings such a beautiful experience to the sitter. Begin by finding a quiet comfortable place and closing your eyes. Take three nice deep breaths and with every exhale allow any tension, any worry, and negativity to be released from your body. Continue to focus your energy inward. Visualize a staircase in front of you and at the top of the staircase you see a door. Start walking up the staircase and as you reach the door, take a moment and set the intention that on the other side of this door, someone you love deeply who has crossed over, is waiting for you. When you open the door, take a look around. You'll find a dining room table close by that invites you to come and get comfortable. As you sit at the table, put your hands out on the table and close your eyes just for a moment. You hear the moving of the chair closest to you and feel your hands being taken lovingly. Go ahead and open your eyes. Your loved one is sitting before you. Rejoice in the reconnection. Tell them how much you love them, how much you miss them, and how your life has been. Be here in this moment. When you are ready to go, say your goodbyes, and start making your way back to the door and down the stairs. Begin bringing yourself back into your physical body and in the room. Know that you can access this stairway anytime.

CHAPTER TEN

LOVE

I was woken up at 3:33am. Since writing this book, I have woken up several times during the early morning hours with not a hint of exhaustion. I have learned to realize this is Spirit's of way of wanting to co-create with me in the writing process. I have a strong connection with my main guide, who is responsible for most of the information and exercises you will find through this chapter. He has been a trusted ally, and an unconditional supporter in the writing process, and in my life. I want to take this time to acknowledge him. Even though he doesn't have a physical body, I know he's real. I know he is there. He comes to me in my thoughts, visions, and feelings. He sits next to me when I am far from my natural state of unconditional love. He stands beside me in all of my earthly celebrations. He is my protector, my guardian, my most trusted confidante.

I share this information with you because I want to remind you... you have your very own angel. You have at least one guide who has watched you grow, learn, and evolve into the beautiful soul you are today. They have listened to your prayers, stood beside you in your times of need, and nurtured you through your growing pains. They see you through the eyes of unconditional love. If you ever want help from your guides, if you ever feel like you have strayed away from love, ask them for a sign. But you must ask.

If you want to strengthen your connection with them, meditation is the gateway that will allow you to quiet your own mind long enough to hear the guidance and love they are eager to give you at this time. I share this information with you because I know what it feels like when you are starting out on your journey and wanting to develop your connection to the Universe. I know how our rational mind tends to go into overdrive when we are stepping outside our comfort zone and attempting to talk to angels and other non-physical beings. Your logical mind will be a great tool and also a pain in the ass. If there is anything I have learned to be true, it is seeing is not believing, believing is seeing.

CONNECT WITH YOUR SPIRIT GUIDES

(Please note: there are many different ways to connect with your spirit guides. The process I am sharing with you below is one that I have personally used and has had tremendous success with using. I hope you enjoy it as much as I did.)

ITEMS NEEDED:

Selenite

Celestine

Rose Quartz

1111 Hz Music (can be found on YouTube)

Earphones

Begin this process lying down in a comfortable place. Before lying down, call upon your guides. You can recite something along the lines of,

"I invite my angels to come co-create with me in this experience. I raise my vibration with the intent to experience love in its purest form. And so it is."

Set a timer on your phone for 30 minutes.

Begin the process by placing the rose quartz near your heart space, celestine on your throat, and selenite at your brow chakra. Lay down and begin playing the music.

This experience will be unique for you. You will receive the experience that is needed to unfold for you. Do not question, nor judge it.

Whenever you feel the absence of love in your life, this is a beautiful way to bring yourself back to it, with the help of your guides.

NATURAL STATE PRAYER

I shine my light freely with no limitations,

I transmute negative into positive,

I rise above,

I am a child of God.

A keeper of light.

I am a co-creator with the universe.

I am my mother's daughter,

My child's mother.

I love with every fiber of my being.

I discard anything that is not for my greatest and highest potential.

I embrace my authentic self with unconditional love and devotion.

I always come back to love.

I fill my heart with gratitude

And my mind with innovation.

I see myself and others in the lens of love.

Love is not something you try to obtain.

Love is a state of universal being.

The only thing that truly exists is love or an absence of it.

In your truest and highest vibration you are love.

This state of being in attainable to all.

It is when you push away from love the human emotional system is then activated.

It is when you make the choice to step closer to fear that love becomes harder to hold.

The frequency of love is within you at all times.

But you mask it with stories you tell yourself that bring you to a lower vibration place.

Fear is only the absence of love.

The lower vibrational states such as anger, pain, guilt, and self-loathing are your indication you have strayed away from your natural state of being, which is love.

When you are at the lower vibrational states love is easily cultivated by peeling off the layers of the stories you tell yourself that distance you from your natural vibrational state of pure love.

Your naked and most authentic self is love. It is the universal consciousness that resides in all. I will now share with you an exercise that will assist you in obtaining a higher vibration and coming back to love.

PEELING THE LAYERS:

Close your eyes and envision yourself as if you are dressed for a cold winter day. Snow boots, long johns, undershirt, sweater, coat, gloves, hat, ear muffs, everything. Underneath these layers lies your natural state of pure unconditional love. Start by taking off a piece of clothing. Look at the piece of clothing and you will see a word written on it. This is what this piece of clothing represents. Take off another piece of clothing and notice the word or story this item represents. Continue peeling off the layers and take note of what each item represents. When you are naked, when you are at your truest and most authentic form, be still. Be in the presence of love. One can use this tool as a reminder when longing for a reconnection back to love.

CHAPTER ELEVEN

ALIGN

It is time to answer the call,

It is time to take radical responsibility for your life.

It is time to heal your inner child,

And embrace the goddess within you.

It is time to reflect,

It is time to step away,

It is time to feel the power rising.

You are exactly where you need to be,

And you are the perfect version of yourself at this exact moment in time.

You do not need permission to step into your own light.

You do not need the approval of others to walk YOUR path.

Your life, your choices, and your beliefs, are exclusive to you.

And only you.

It is time to align.

It is time to rise.

Motivation versus discipline

When it comes to completely changing your life, you have to remember [and constantly remind yourself] there is a difference between motivation and actual implementation and incorporation. Motivation is easy to come by, whether it's following your favorite coaches and healers on Instagram, scrolling through Pinterest, reading a self-help book, listening to a bomb ass girl power anthem like *Blank Space, Sorry Not Sorry,* or *Thank U* next. Motivation is easy to come by.

How many times have you felt inspired, uplifted, and ready to take on the world? How many stories have you heard throughout the years that have made you say to yourself,

"If they can do it, I can do it."

How many times have you watched *The Secret* documentary and became obsessed with the Law of Attraction and felt motivation to start visualizing your dream life? Turning the key and starting the engine is the easy part. The actual work is when you actually have to drive to the destination. And I hate to be the bearer of bad news, but the drive has a 99% chance of not being a smooth one. You are going to have many roadblocks, sometimes detours, and you are definitely going to have asshole drivers who are only there to test you.

Motivation is free of charge,

Discipline comes with an expense.

You are going to mess up. You are going to be put in tough situations. You are going to pushed into corners. You are going to want to throw temper tantrums. You are going to be misunderstood, taken advantage of, and ridiculed. You are going to feel like shit sometimes. But you are not going to give up. You are going to take every uncomfortable obstacle and you are going to find the lesson embedded within it. You are going to take these lessons and you are going to learn from them and you are going to be become a wiser, stronger version of yourself.

HINDSIGHT IS 20/20

Take your journal or a piece of paper, and I want you to write out 3-5 big, impactful experiences you have already encountered in your life. It doesn't matter what these experiences were. Anything that really rattled you or left you feeling less than or not enough. Once you have collected your thoughts, sit up straight and close your eyes. Take three deep breaths in and place both your hands over your heart. Send out an invitation in your thoughts to invite your angels and guides to help you in this exercise. Envision a beautiful ball of light in the center of your chest expanding. Once you feel this power emanating from your chest, state out loud,

"I choose to see the light, I choose to see the lessons."

And gradually open your eyes. See these experiences with a new, clearer set of eyes. Go through each experience and write down the lessons that naturally come to mind for each event. Don't judge or rationalize what comes through. Just allow it to flow through you. You might be surprised at what comes through or it may make total and complete sense to you. This exercise isn't for you to judge, it's for you to have an opportunity to see the lessons that lay in the madness.

It is called TRANSFORM for a reason.

If you want to transform your life, then you have to TRANSFORM YOUR LIFE. You have to do the work. You have to remember that you, as bright and smart and intelligent as you are, decided to be human. You decided on this life, this gender, and believe it or not, you chose your parents. You chose your siblings, and also at the soul level, chose some of your friends. You are not the victim of your circumstances; you are the wise soul that chose these mountains to climb because you know how innately capable you are of doing so. You are the lightworker who decided to come down at this point in history to help raise the collective vibration. You are the soul your children willingly chose as their mother. You are the soul who knows when you heal yourself, you heal others.

You might be thinking to yourself that, 'She's a little rough around the edges.'

That I'm not like other self help/spirituality writers that inspire, and empower, and uplift. And to be honest, you are 100% correct.

The truth is, I don't want to inspire you.

I want to wake you up.

I'm here to help you remember.

One guided meditation isn't going to change your life,

Nor is reading one spiritual or self-help book.

Holding a rose quartz crystal isn't going to give you the self- love you desire unless you are willing to cultivate self-love within YOURSELF first.

Holding a black tourmaline crystal isn't going to protect your energy if you are in a toxic environment and/or relationship. You have to become aware of your present circumstances and start making changes that will put you in a better, safer place both physically and mentally before the protective energy of black tourmaline will do the work.

The transformation, the new upgraded version of yourself, begins with you DECIDING you are worthy of better.

You get to decide your quality of life.

You get to decide what you allow within your life.

You get to decide how people treat you.

You get to decide your boundaries.

You get to decide what is important to you.

And most importantly, you get to decide what your spirituality looks like.

There has never been a better time for you to choose YOU.

There has never been a better to time to begin hearing the whispers of your soul and the guidance of Spirit.

Trust that Spirit is continuously working with you, guiding you, supporting you, and encouraging you.

Trust yourself and the internal guidance that is readily available to you.

And as our good friend Winnie the Pooh said,

"You are braver than you believe,

Stronger than you seem,

Smarter than you think,

And loved more than you will ever know."

Where to go from here

For online courses, mentorship, trainings, and more, head to

www.ericarusso.co

FREE RESOURSES:

Intuitive Souls Podcast — My podcast that gives you tips, tricks, and grounded practical tools to help you live your life with intuition and intention. Available on iTunes, Stitcher, google play, I Heart Radio, and all major podcast platforms.

15 Tools to Develop your Intuition: Grab the list of my favorite 15 tools to develop your intuition at www.ericarusso.co

Follow me on Social Media:

Instagram: @ericawrusso

TikTok: @ericawrusso

Facebook: @EricaWRusso

ACKNOWLEDGMENTS

My husband Tony, my best friend, my #1 fan, and my rock.

My sons, Nathan & Kyle for helping me see the world through your eyes. Meg V, for your relentless and unwavering support and believing in me. My cousin Sam, you inspire me more than you know. Sonya B – for the mug and the push I needed (it's like you're psychic or something!) My family, my mom and dad, brother and sister, and for everyone who's a part of the Intuitive Life Society.

Made in the USA
Las Vegas, NV
15 February 2022